Plants and People

Karnataka Rites of Passage

by

Suzanne Hanchett

with contributions by

Stanley Regelson and K. Gurulingaiah

Development Resources Press, Pasadena, California

Library of Congress Control Number: 2022923558

Plants and People; Karnataka Rites of Passage Bibliography, Glossary

1. Ethnobotany–India, 2. Rituals–Hindu folk, 3. Rites of Passage, 4. Kinship system–Dravidian, 5. Social Sciences–Anthropology, 6. Religion and beliefs

ISBN 979-8-9868769-5-5 (e-book)

ISBN 979-8-9868769-4-8 (paperback)

Contents

PREFACE 1

INTRODUCTION 3

    Ethnobotany in India 7

PART I 11

    CUSTOMARY USES OF PLANT MATERIALS IN FAMILY
    RITUALS 11

    RITES OF PASSAGE 14

    Birth, Cradle, and Naming Rituals 14

        Birth and cradle rituals 14

        Naming rituals 19

        Foods brought to the birth house after one month 23

        Summary: Plants in Birth and Naming Rituals 24

    Maturation Rituals for Girls 28

        Summary: Plants in Girl's Maturation Rituals 36

    Initiation Rituals for Boys 40

        Non-Brahman Daasayya Initiation Rituals 42

        Brahman and Smith Caste Sacred Thread Ceremonies 46

        Summary 52

    Marriage Rituals 57

        Bringing waters to witness the marriage 62

        Preliminary ceremonies for the bride 66

        Preliminary ceremonies for the bridegroom 70

        Grinding and pounding food grains 74

        The bridegroom's arrival 75

        Creating the marriage bond (*muhurta, muhurtam,* or *dhaare*) 78

        The wedding canopy 85

        Ritual exchanges after a marriage 85

        Summary: Plants in Marriage Rituals 86

Pregnancy Rituals...93

  Summary: Plants in Seventh Month Pregnancy Rituals................95
  Rituals Associated with Death and Widowhood............................99

    The day of a death 101
    Going to the burial or cremation place 104
    Burial, cremation, and widowhood rituals.....................105
    Transition of a 'married woman' (*muTTayide*) to the status of
    widow:...110
    Rituals performed soon after a death..............................110
    Rituals on the 11th day, concluding the period of ritual pollution 114
    Rituals for deceased children..119
    Summary: Plants and Plant Parts in Death Rituals.......121
  FEEDING COOKED RICE TO THE ANCESTORS 129
  APPEASING DANGEROUS SPIRITS 137
PART II...145

  REVIEW AND SUMMARY 145
  The Most Commonly Used Plants in Family Rituals....................145

    Coconut (*Cocos nucifera*)...146
    Plantain (*Musa sapientum*) 148
    Turmeric (*Curcuma longa*)..148
    Betel leaves (*Piper betle*) 149
    Areca (*Areca catechu*)..151
    Bengal gram (*Cicer arietinum*) 152
    Rice (*Oryza sativa*)..152
    Rice in Auspicious Rituals 153
    Mango leaves..154
  Symbolic Uses of Some Other Plants and Plant Parts...................155

    Flowering plants and flowers 155
    Garlands..155
    Cassia fistula and Calotropis gigantea............................156
    Leucas indica..157
    Vegetables 158
    Seed Grains, Grams, Pulses, and Buds...........................159
    Two Grasses 161
    Sticks and Branches...161
    The Sacred Fig Tree 163
PART III...165

  DISCUSSION AND CONCLUSIONS 165
  Discussion 165

Conclusions 173

REFERENCES AND BIBLIOGRAPHY 175

ANNEX -1 187

  CASTE AND SUBCASTE NAMES 187
ANNEX-2 188

  INTERVIEW WITH AN *AYNORU* PRIEST............................ 188
ANNEX-3 189

  BECOMING A BRAHMAN WIDOW: THEN AND NOW 189
    1976 Explanation by an Iyengar Woman 189
ANNEX-4 193

  FOLK TAXONOMY: PLANT CATEGORIES AND PLANT PARTS
.... 193

    Categories of Plants.. 194

    Named Plant Parts 196

ANNEX-5 205

  TRANSCRIPTION OF KANNADA WORDS............................. 205
ANNEX-6 206

  GLOSSARY OF BOTANICAL AND KANNADA PLANT NAMES 206
AUTHOR BIOGRAPHIES... 215

Tables

Table 1. Plant Materials in Birth, Cradle, and Naming Rituals.............. 25

Table 2. Uses of Specific Plants in Girls' Maturation Rituals 37

Table 3. Named Combinations of Plant Items in Girls' Maturation Rituals
.... 39

Table 4. Plant Materials Used in Boys' Initiation Rituals.................... 54

Table 5. Symbolic Uses of Plant Materials in Marriage Rituals 88

Table 6. Plant Materials Used in Seventh Month Pregnancy Rituals........ 97

Table 7. Plant Materials Used in Death Rituals 123

Table 8. Plant Materials Used in Ancestor Ceremonies.................... 134

Table 9. Plant Materials Forbidden in Many Ancestor Ceremonies 135

Table 10. Plant Materials Associated with Restless *Amma* Spirits 143

Photos, Drawings, Diagrams

Figure 1. A Winnowing Fan, the First Bed of a Newborn Infant (photo of a miniature) 17

Figure 2. An Infant Just Moved to Its Cradle, with plantain leaf and rice set below it 18

Figure 3. Offerings to the Place of a Birth, Scheduled Caste, Bandipur ... 18

Figure 4. Putting *baj-beNNe* in the Mouth of a New Baby, Scheduled Caste, Bandipur 19

Figure 5. A Typical *hase maNe* Wooden Platform 19

Figure 6. Farmer Caste Girl in Her Leaf Shed 33

Figure 7. Maternal Uncle of Farmer Caste Girl Coming out of Her Leaf Shed (Bandipur, 1967 33

Figure 8. Lap-filling Ceremony for a Scheduled Caste Girl (Bandipur) ... 33

Figure 9. Brahman Boy Getting a Shave from a Local Barber (Bandipur Village, 1967) 53

Figure 10. Brahman Boy with His Father and a Priest at a Sacred Fig Tree (Chinnapura Village, 1967) 53

Figure 11. Iyengar Brahman Boy (L) and an Initiated Companion, with branches of bastard teak, on their way to the sacred fig tree (Bandipur, 1967) 54

Figure 12. Boy and His Companion at the Sacred Fig Tree: Branch of Bastard Teak set into the trunk of the tree (Bandipur, 1967) ... 54

Figure 13. *Daasayya* Officiating at a Scheduled Caste Wedding, Bandipur 59

Figure 14. Scheduled Caste Musicians, Bandipur 59

Figure 15. Filling *airaNe* Vessels at the River. Shepherd caste wedding, Chinnapura 1967 63

Figure 16. Carrying *airaNe* Vessels back from the River: Scheduled Caste Wedding, Chinnapura 1967 63

Figure 17. *airaNe* Vessels in a Farmer Caste Wedding House, with a Bunch of Areca Flowers. (Chinnapura, 1967) 64

Figure 18. Drawing of a Temple Cart on Wall Above *airaNes*. Farmer caster wedding, Chinnapura 1967 65

Figure 19. Pounding Paddy Before a Marriage (Scheduled Caste, Chinnapura, 1967) 69

Figure 20. Iyengar Bride Seated in front of a Grinding Stone before Her Marriage (Bandipur, 1966) 69

Figure 21. An Iyengar Bride Putting on New Glass Bangles (Bandipur, 1966) 69

Figure 22. Three Small Cubes of Jaggery, called *chiTTAchu* (courtesy of Nikita Chandan) 69

Figure 23. A Bridegroom, Bringing a Sari, Areca Flowers, and Other Items, is Welcomed at the Bride's House (Weaver caste, 1967) 81

Figure 24. Pouring Milk and Clarified Butter over the Newly Married Couples' Hands (Weaver caste, Bandipur, 1967) 81

Figure 25. Curtain Separating the Bride and Groom, just before they exchange garlands (Weaver caste, Bandipur, 1967) 81

Figure 26. *Phala Puja* with Tender Coconuts and Areca Flowers. Farmer Caste Wedding, Chinnapura 1967 82

Figure 27. Widow Seated to the Left of Her Deceased Husband. Oil Presser caste funeral, Bandipur, 1966 103

Figure 28. Washing the Corpse Before the Public Viewing. Oil Presser caste, Bandipur, 1966 103

Figure 29. A Nephew of the Deceased Man Cries Loudly, as friends and relatives offer *puja*: Fisherman caste, Bandipur, 1966 104

Figure 30. A Caste-mate Offers a Final Incense-stick *puja* to the Deceased Man: Fisherman caste, Bandipur, 1966 104

Figure 31. Mourners Bathing at the River after the Burial. Fisherman caste funeral, Bandipur 107

Figure 32. Woman Prostrating to the Grave. Fisherman caste funeral, Bandipur 107

Figure 33. *Leucas indica* Plant (source: https://commons.wikim edia.org/wiki/File: Leucas_aspera_plant.jpg#/media/File:aLeucas_aspera_plant.jpg) 108

Figure 34. Procession to the Grave. Fisherman caste funeral, Bandipur. 108

Figure 35. Setting a *Leucas indica* Plant in the Path to the Grave(Bandipur, Oil Presser funeral) 108

Figure 36. *Chakra* Made by Aynoru Priest (diagram from author's field notes) 115

Figure 37. Farmer House Ancestor Offering, Bandipur 1966 132

Figure 38. 'Married Woman' *kaLasha* (drawing by Carol Francis, from a photograph) 132

Figure 39. Ancestor Meals Offered in a Scheduled Caste Home (from a drawing by H. Bettaiah, Bandipur 1967) 132

Figure 40. Bitter Gourd (*Momordica charantia*), a Common Requirement 133

Figure 41. *Luffa acutangula*: Not Served to Ancestors (Photo Source: By Nayan j Nath - Own work, CC BY-SA 4.0, https://commons.wikim edia.org/w/index .php?c urid=122715168) 133

Figure 42. *Hibiscus esculentis*: Not Served to Ancestors 133

Figure 43. Bottle Gourd (*Lagenaria siseraria*), a Common Requirement for Ancestor Meals 133

Figure 44. Outdoor Meal Offered to Goddess Piriyapattanadamma 139

Figure 45. Ancestral-type Offering to Goddess Mastiamma at an Outdoor Shrine 140

Figure 46. *Nerium indicum:* Kannada *kaNigal huuvu* 140

Figure 47. *Plumeria rubra* flower, *Kannada deyya kaNigal huuvu* 140

Figure 48. Calotropis gigantea flower: Kannada, (y)ekkadahuuvu (https://commons.wikimedia.org/wiki/File:Calotropis_gigantea_ in_Belur_Math,_Howrah,_West_Bengal.jpg#/media/File:Calotr opis_gigantea_in_Belur_Math,_Howrah,_West_Bengal.jpg) 140

Figure 49. *Calotropis gigantea* Plant (https://commons.wikimedia.org/wiki/File:Ankhada_Plant_with _full_bloom.jpg#/media/ File:Ankhada_Plant_with_full_bloom.jpg) 141

Figure 50. Five *kaT* (tied packets) of Betel Leaves, on a Plate with Plantains (upper left). Weaver caste wedding, Bandipur 1967 (photo by Doranne Jacobson, International Images) 147

Figure 51. Botanical Drawing of Coconut Tree, and Fruit with and without the endocarp 147

Figure 52. Powdered Turmeric, Sold at the Weekly Village Market, Bandipur 1976 147

Figure 53. Betel Leaf *kankaNa* on Bridegroom's Wrist, Bandipur 1967 (photo by Doranne Jacobson, International Images) 147

Figure 54: Coconut Flowers   (Kannada, *hombaaLe* 151

Figure 55. Turmeric-colored Rice (akšate) in the Hair of a Scheduled Caste
Bride, Bandipur, 1967 151

Figure 56. Areca Flowers (Kannada, *hombaaLe*) 151

Figure 57. String of Mango Leaves on a House Door, for an auspicious
event (Bandipur, 1967) 154

Figure 58. Sacred Fig Tree with Platform at Village Entrance 163

Figure 59. An Elderly Widow Drying Her Red Sari Near the River,
Bandipur 1966 192

Figure 60. Named Parts of a Plant 197

Figure 61. Named Parts of a Tree 198

Figure 62. Types of Leaves 199

Figure 63. Plantain Leaf Parts 199

Figure 64. Spathe of a Palm Frond 202

Figure 65. Named Parts of a Flower 203

PREFACE

The research on which this book is based was conducted by me, together with Dr. Stanley Regelson and an excellent group of research assistants in two villages of Hassan District, Karnataka State, India. We spent 21 months doing ethnographic research while living in the villages in 1966-1967; and I did another four months of fieldwork in 1976 and 1977 focusing on ethnobotany issues. Our ethnographic research was funded by the U.S. National Institute of Mental Health (mine) and the National Science Foundation (Stanley Regelson's). My ethnobotany studies were funded by the American Institute of Indian Studies and a Fulbright Faculty Research Abroad grant. Much of the initial data analysis was facilitated by an Ogden Mills Fellowship at the American Museum of Natural History (1969-70) and a fellowship from the American Council of Learned Societies (1975).

I am especially grateful to our assistant, Mr. K. Gurulingaiah, who conducted interviews with members of multiple castes about the ways that they conducted their rites of passage. Dr. Regelson and I were able to observe some of these events, and K. Gurulingaiah's interviews provided details on the ritual requirements of all castes. Mrs. Joyce George, H. Malathi, Malla Setty, and G.P. Jayamma, my interpreters and assistants, also helped greatly with all aspects of this work. In 1976 and 1977, a Bangalore botanist, Dr. (Rev.) Cecil J. Saldanha, helped with botanical identifications of many of the plants discussed here.

Dr. Helen Ullrich, Shalini R. Bhat, Mr. Malla Setty, and Dr. Narayan Hegde were most helpful with review of this manuscript and checking Kannada spellings. The Kannada terms used here are those known to be in use in Hassan District at the time of the research.

INTRODUCTION

Plants have been important in South Asian culture for at least three millennia. The leaf of the sacred fig (*Ficus religiosa*) -- also known as the Bo tree, under which the Buddha sat and attained enlightenment – was an element in the ancient Harappan script. Jain philosophers included plants in their early discourses on the soul. Floral motifs are inscribed in the walls of Hindu, Jain, and other temples, and living flowers can be found for ritual uses in their gardens. (Gupta 2001, Jain and Jain 2020)

Mythology and poetry over the centuries have made ample use of plant imagery. The puranic tale of the *parijata* flower, which is said to shed gold in the garden of its keeper, and for which Satyabamma went to war, has been revived in a Kannada story, *Sri Krishna Paarijaata*.[1] Though Satyabamma won the plant prize and planted it in her garden, its gold fell only into the neighboring garden of her co-wife Rukmeni.

In his comparison of Sanskrit and classical Tamil poetry, George Hart (1975) illustrates the extensive use they both make of plants. Intertwined plants, plants shedding their flowers, plants trampled in battle, plants slowly dying - images such as these form metaphoric equations between plant life and human experience. A.K. Ramanujan's description of Tamil *Sangam* poetic conventions shows five landscapes being distinguished according to the specific flower or tree typical of

---

[1] Available at https://archive.org/details/sri-krishna-parijata/page/n1/mode/2up

each of them. These landscapes are the settings for five distinct personal moods; and their plants are used as metonymic shorthand for the five phases of lovers' relationships: union, separation, patient waiting, anxious waiting, and infidelity and resentment.[2]

Plants appear also in songs and proverbs. A saying in our research area, for example, was, "If you see the *lakke* flower [*Vitex negundo*], at least give her a *namaskaara*." The fact that some figs have very small flowers receives attention in some common Indian sayings about them. Abbott (1974) reports that fig trees are said to fruit without flowering at all. Margaret Trawick mentions a Tamil proverb that compares meeting a hard-to-find person with the difficulty of seeing a fig tree flowering.[3]

One Karnataka flower, the *tumbe* (*Leucas indica*), has the shape of a foot, so the devotee Baderakanappa, hero of a movie popular in the 1960s and 1970s, expresses his eternal deference to Siva ('Your foot is on my head') by using it in worship. The *paarijaata* flower (*Nyctanthes arbor-tristis*) sheds its flowers easily, so the Kannda novelist Masti Venkatesh Iyengar uses it in his book, *Subbanna* (1943), to stand for a man's vulnerability:

> [A young bride remembers her mother's words of wisdom as she tries not to inflict the evil eye on her husband:] "Man is like the flower of the *parijat*. To look steadily at him is to wither him." Looking fully at Subbanna for a moment Lalithamma remembered this dictum and turned her eyes away. (p. 29)

---

[2] Ramanujan 1967
[3] Margaret Trawick Egnor, personal communication (1979)

Popular sayings and customs endow some trees with maternal and feminine qualities:

> Analogies of flowering and fruiting trees with females abound. Popular Tamil songs liken barren women to trees that do not fruit, and a common term for menstruation is Puttal or flowering. The resemblance of the white sap produced by some trees, including pipal, to milk gives rise to a practice of sympathetic magic. Owners of cows place the placentas of newly born calves into bags which they tie to branches of trees that extrude this milky sap. The tree 'feeds' the placenta in the same way as a cow feeds her calf. (Venkatesan 2021:481)

Trees may be "married" to people. They can also be married to each other. One environmentally-oriented article (John 2017) on tree marriage in Kerala State describes a full wedding ceremony (with formal invitations, *taaLi*-tying, garlanding, and so on) between a banyan tree (*Ficus indica*) and a mango tree (*Mangifera indica*). This author quotes an environmental activist, who said that, "By carrying out this interesting ritual we also want to say that trees are living beings who have feelings. Awareness on the need to protect trees can also be created through such traditions."

In another, more detailed article Soumhya Venkatesan describes a Tamil village marriage between a sacred fig/*pipal* tree and a neem tree (*Azadirachta indica*). A Brahmin priest officiating at the marriage explained the practice:

> Souls (atman) have to take bodies to spend karma accrued in previous embodied births. Once a soul has zero karma (i.e. performs no consequential actions that require rebirth), it can

5

attain liberation (moksha) from the cycle of birth and rebirth (samsara). Some souls might have a last karmic duty left to fulfil and so take a final body. This last body ideally is one that will not accrue more karma. Trees make good last bodies because trees do not act intentionally; no karma attaches to their actions of giving shade, fruit, and so on.

When a neem and a pipal tree grow close together, Mahesh told me, it is said that they are the bodies of advanced souls whose last karmic duty is to undergo marriage. When you wed the trees to each other, you enable the liberation of the souls therein. (Venkatesan 2021:479)

This author commented that, "Throughout India, the pipal is associated with the gods Shiva, Vishnu, and Hanuman. Pipal trees are often found in temples to these deities. The neem is most commonly considered a form of the goddess Shakti."

Studying folk knowledge and practices involving trees around India, Dr. Shakti M. Gupta observed that,

In Orissa if a man loses two wives in succession, before he can be married for the third time, he is married to a tree of *Streblus asper* or *Morus* before he is considered free of the curse of becoming a widower again, as the ill-luck is now carried by the tree he is married to. (Gupta 2001:xxiii) [italics added][4]

---

[4] In the Karnataka region where we did our fieldwork, it is the custom of some castes to perform a marriage on behalf of the spirit of a boy who has died before marrying. This marriage, according to our notes, is conducted between two other boys, one serving as a stand-in for the deceased child, shortly before his next

According to the anthropologists who compiled *The Mysore Tribes and Castes*, many tribes and clans of South India – some of whom eventually became castes -- once thought of specific plants, animals, or inanimate objects as totemic ancestors[5]. Among the plants mentioned in this source, some are quite important in the religious/ritual life of our study area.[6] (Ananthakrishna Iyer 1935:255)

Ethnobotany in India

Ethnobotany has been defined by S.K. Jain as "all aspects of direct relationship of plants with man." (Jain 1995:1) Ethnobotany has greatly expanded in India during the past 40 - 50 years. A most significant endeavor by professional botanists has been the work of the Botanical Survey of India under the leadership of Dr. S. K. Jain and others. This group has produced a large number of articles describing the understandings and uses of plants in tribal, rural, and even urban areas of India. Dr. S. K. Jain himself repeatedly has urged his colleagues to attend to the common names of the plants they study in the field. In his 1996 article on "Transforming Ethnobotany for the New Millennium," Michael Balick notes an important broadening of the concept:

> The discipline of ethnobotany is currently evolving both in its philosophical underpinnings and methodology. (p.65). There is a deep, often spiritual relationship between plants and people, in both traditional settings and among more

---

brother's actual marriage.

[5] Some tribal groups still observe this tradition.

[6] Banyan, Pipal, Mango, Bastard teak, Coconut, Areca, Screw pine, Bamboo, Rice paddy, Plantain, and Turmeric, for example.

7

acculturated societies. These relationships can be elucidated through ethnobotanical studies and used to increase biological literacy among the non-scientific community (p. 65)

In India this change has had far-reaching consequences, as public education and other programs have sharpened attention on environmental issues. Balick mentions that, "Reserves for protecting medicinal plants recently have been established across India, in a nationwide effort to ensure the supply of these important species."(65) Ann Grodzins Gold (2002) has done research in Rajasthan on school children's increasing awareness of the importance of trees to air quality and other benefits.

Shakti M. Gupta's *Plant Myths and Traditions* (2001) is a helpful review of mythology and lore associated with some important symbolic plants. Dr. Gupta, a botanist, has also conducted field interviews in rural areas. Another early effort was organized by Sankar Sen Gupta, who edited a book titled *Tree Symbol Worship* (1965). This collection of writings by folklorists was an important first step in describing the varieties of belief and practice relating to plants.

Ayurvedic medicine may well be associated with symbolic uses of plants, considering the prominent role of plants in this ancient science. Zimmerman has referred to Ayurveda as a "vegetarian" medical system because of the extensive uses it makes of plants and refined herbal products.[7] As Basham points out, "Indian medicine had 'an intuitive genius and actual command of the details of its environment. That intuitive genius expressed itself particularly in efficient surgical

---

[7] Zimmerman 1978:183

techniques and a deep understanding of the pharmacopoeia provided *by* the abundant flora and fauna of India." [19] Ayurveda is associated with the magical Atharva Veda as a secondary science. Caraka, one of its earliest systematizers, divided it into eight branches, one of which was "pharmaceutics." A basic text by Sushruta mentions seven hundred medicinal plants. Work in contemporary laboratories, small clinics, and in home remedies is still expanding on this knowledge and relating it to Western medical sciences.

The relationship between Ayurveda and common plant knowledge is one of mutual exchange. Basham states that some texts [*e.g.* Sushruta i:36.10] advise the *vaidya* [practitioner] to gain knowledge of unusual herbal remedies from hillmen, herdsmen, and forest-dwelling hermits."[8] And he speculates that tribal peoples of India's hills must have been actively contributing to Ayurvedic pharmacopoeias for many centuries: "Though not mentioned directly there must have been a considerable trade in drugs from the mountains to the plains, and also from the humid tropical hills of the peninsula, where many herbs grew which would not thrive in the drier north, with its cool winters."[9] These observations suggest that plants thought to have magical powers may find their way into the traditional doctor's bag of remedies, as well as medicinal plants finding their way into folklore. Some of the ritual plants with which I am concerned are also used as Ayurvedic medicines[10].

[8] Basham 1976:27

[9] Basham 1976:30. The work of the Botanical Survey of India, especially S.K. Jain's research, focuses on tribal ethnobotany to a large extent. It would be interesting to compare the patterning of life form classes and of tribal and peasant taxonomies.

[10] Mark Nichter's research on Ayurvedic medicine in South Kanara District, for example, found that some plants I observed being used in pregnancy rituals and a goddess ceremony of Iyengars are also used in birth and pregnancy disorders.

9

Doing 1966-67 ethnographic research for my Ph.D. dissertation in two villages of Hassan District, Karnataka State, together with Dr. Stanley Regelson, I became intrigued by the artistry of folk rites. These customs express people's hopes for family health, continuity, and good fortune as they attempt to bless their children's progress in life, or to please deities and ancestors assumed to influence family destinies. The rituals always involve manipulation of numerous colorful and interesting items as offerings, decorations, or expressions of blessing. Commonplace things – vessels, foods, powders, fruits, and flowers -- are used in folk Hindu ritual *(puja)* offerings expressing people's wishes for their families to thrive. Plant materials are prominent among the things required (or tabooed) for rites of passage and offerings to deities -- specific types of leaves, fruits, flowers, twigs, branches, and so on. I included some of this information in my book about four types of family-centered festivals, *Coloured Rice; Symbolic Structure in Hindu Family Festivals* (Hanchett 2023)[11].

Thirty-one of his list of medicinal plants are in my group of symbolic plants.

[11] *Coloured Rice* was originally published in 1988. The second edition of this book is available in print on www.amazon.com or as an e-book from www.devresbooks.com.

PART I

CUSTOMARY USES OF PLANT
MATERIALS IN FAMILY RITUALS

During our ethnographic research in two Karnataka villages in 1966 and 1967, Stanley Regelson and I observed many community festivals and private rituals – in temples, in fields, in village streets, and in homes. They were important to the public life of each village as a whole,[12] and they provided every family with ways to manage family transitions. There are commonly agreed ways of doing things at the whole-village level: coordinated groups pushing and pulling a temple cart with an important deity seated atop it around the village streets, for example.

Each group has its own specific ways of fending off spiritual danger, celebrating beloved deities, or getting their members born and named, matured, married, and buried. Within this variety of practice, certain common patterns can be found. A fixed 'requirement' to do a certain ritual action is referred to as *shaastra*. We found that different castes or subcastes may agree on these basic 'requirements', even if their celebrations vary greatly in other details. There also are prohibitions against using certain plants, flowers, or leaves, etc. on

---

[12] Hanchett 1970 discusses the ways in which one village festival served as an opportunity for conflicting factions to resolve their differences after land reform legislation had been passed in India.

11

some occasions. Focusing on both requirements and prohibitions can help us to decipher at least some of the meanings within this complex and dazzling variety of objects and actions. It reveals some degree of continuity in a sphere of action where there seems to be no one system.

Asking directly about the meanings of *shaastras*, we rarely got interesting answers. Asked why a Diipaavali (Divali) broom should be made only of certain types of plants and not others, for example, we were often told that these are merely 'customs' (*paddhati*) with no obvious moral or spiritual meanings. Priests, other religious specialists, and soothsayers have had some role in guiding these practices, but many probably have been passed down from one generation to another, mixing tradition with invention.

A central question guiding this study is, How and why are specific plant items used (or tabooed) in certain family rituals? Some of the 50+ plants discussed below, such as the sacred fig and neem trees, show up in numerous Indian ethnobotany studies, but others seem to have come into usage for reasons buried in the history of oral traditions.Characteristics of the plants themselves and mythological associations are well known to make them suitable for ritual uses. The three-leaf growth pattern of the *patre* type of plant, for example, was actually mentioned as an auspicious feature supporting its use in some rites. Five is also an auspicious number. Certain colors (white, yellow, red, or black especially) are considered to lend an auspicious or inauspicious quality to an event. Plants that grow as vines are favored as foods in ancestor feasts. (Hanchett 2023) The sacred basil plant (*tuLasi*) is worthy of worship because it is believed to incarnate the spirit of a virtuous woman who protected her husband's life.

Other plants' possible meanings are more elusive. Despite people's general reluctance to make meanings explicit, this study arises from an assumption that ritual items probably do reflect certain values or emotions, though the symboling process is largely unconscious. In this rituals resemble other arts, such as music, which can speak to us of things that may be difficult to express in words.

Some plants used symbolically are eaten, and some are not. The focus here is on symbolic uses of plants, rather than on their role as cooked foods. However, as cooking is itself a very meaningful act in this way of life, plants can become symbolically important when specific vegetable preparations are required (*"shaastra"*), especially in ceremonies for ancestors .

In the next section I will explore the ways that specific plants and plant parts are deployed in rites of passage and other ceremonies with special importance to families. Most of our detailed information on these rituals was gathered by a team consisting of myself, Stanley Regelson, K. Gurulingaiah, Malla Setty, and several other research assistants in 1966 and 1967. I did some supplementary research focused on ethnobotany in 1976 and 1977. The two villages in which we did our ethnographic study are located in Hassan District, Karnataka. We refer to them as "Bandipur" and "Chinnapura," which are fictitious names.

RITES OF PASSAGE

Birth, Cradle, and Naming Rituals

Our information on birth, cradle and naming rituals comes from interviews with members of 10 different castes and sub-castes[13] and direct observations in the homes of four different groups.

Birth and cradle rituals

Almost all castes customarily keep a newborn infant in a winnowing fan (*moRa*) for a while after birth. Moving it to a cradle (on the third, fifth, seventh, or ninth day after birth) is a special ritual, called *guNige shaastra*, involving some local celebration and possibly distribution of **betel-areca** sets and other items, such as **ripe plantains,** to friends and family members. According to a local midwife, a **coconut** is broken soon after a birth, in order to avoid the 'evil eye' (*drišti*) harming the mother or child. An important plant item for almost all non-Brahman castes is a mixture of **nutmeg** (*Myristica fragrans*) and butter (Kannada *bajbeNNe*), of which a small amount is put into the baby's mouth.[14]

A Farmer (Daas Okkaliga) caste ritual includes tossing a mixture of **finger millet, unhusked paddy, and horse gram** (*huraLikaaLu*).[15]

---

[13] Scheduled Caste (A.K.), Washerman, Weaver, Barber, Oil Presser, Iyengar Brahman, Smith, Farmer (three subcastes), Smartha Brahman, and Fisherman.

[14] *baje* is the Kannada term for *Acorus calamus* (sweet flag). It is given as medicine to new mothers. Our notes do not indicate whether this is part of the *baj-beNNe* mixture, but the name suggests that it may be.

[15] *Eleusine coracana* (finger millet), *Oryza sativa* (rice), and *Macrotyloma uniflorumc*(horse gram)

The new mother's maternal uncle (*sodarmaava*), with a small piece of **jaggery** in his mouth and a special thread tied to his leg, takes an offering to the Maramma Shrine. As he returns to the house, he scatters *accande* – the mixture of millet, paddy, and gram – along the way.

Back at the house, he goes three times around the winnowing fan that the baby had been kept in and ties the thread from his leg around the waist of the baby. He then puts a mixture of **nutmeg** and butter (*baj-beNNe*) into the baby's mouth. Then the new mother, the baby's father, and the baby's grandparents – all also put the mixture into the baby's mouth. The baby is now ready to go into the cradle. **Betel-areca** and **sugar** are distributed to all those present. An insect (of any type) is buried in a small hole at the spot where the birth took place. (K. Gurulingaiah notes, 9 October 1967)

In one Scheduled Caste cradle ceremony we observed a bundle of the same mixture – **millet, paddy, and horse gram,** called *daanya* in this community – wrapped in a **tamarind-juice** soaked cloth and tied by the new mother with a special string (*hasinulu*) to the side of the new baby's cradle. A Farmer caste man told us that the baby stays in its winnowing fan for 10 days. When he/she is moved to the cradle, a male relative (perhaps the child's mother's father) sprinkles the mixture of **millet, paddy, and horse gram** around the winnowing fan in which the baby has stayed until then. The meaning of this was said to be that, "The child will have enough food throughout its whole life." After this **sugar** and **betel-areca** are distributed to those present, an evening dinner will be arranged for all relatives. A member of another

Farmer group, the Gangadikara Okkaligas, told us that the **same mixture** is circled three times around the inverted winnowing fan after the baby is named, so that "the child will be a successful farmer throughout life."

One Smartha Brahman woman mentioned giving a mixture of **crushed coconut flower** (*hombaaLe*) and milk to a new mother soon after birth. This is intended to promote her health, so it is not technically a "symbolic" gesture, but it deserves mention because the coconut flower figures prominently in inauspicious death rites. The grandmother of this same house told me, when I came to view her daughter's new baby, that "**sugar** is *shaastra*" on this occasion. So she presented me with some **sugar** and **betel-areca**.

In one Iyengar Brahman cradle ceremony we observed, the new mother's own mother put a set of items onto a **plantain leaf** underneath the cradle. The leaf was covered with **raw rice**, and she put on it five sets of betel-areca plus some salted **Bengal gram** (*uppu kaDale*). A small, cow dung mound representing the God Vigneshwara was set in the middle of this and decorated with **turmeric** and vermillion powder. Two brass lamps were lit, and the new mother's sister sang a song. A **coconut** was cracked by smashing it onto a small decorated rock with a religious image (*naama*) painted on it. The grandmother set the rock into the foot-end of the cradle and then handed it to another woman, who handed it back, and she then put the rock into the cradle. The naked baby was circled three times around in the same manner as the rock, but in the opposite direction. The baby was then set in its mother's lap, and the grandmother waved a plate of red liquid *(aarati)*[16] for the new mother and baby. After the baby was finally set into the cradle, guests were given **turmeric** and vermillion powder, together with leaf cups containing a mixture called *kaDale husli* (**whole Bengal gram, shredded dry coconut**, and a fried seasoning mixture called *(v)ogreNNe*).

In a separate interview with an Iyengar Brahman villager, the married women who decorated the cradle (their cradle ceremony was on the same day that the baby was named) werevsaid to be rewarded with a special mixture called *sunDal*, made from boiled or fried **Bengal gram**, salt, grated **coconut**, and seasonings.

A Farmer caste (Mull Okkaliga subcaste) woman told us that the place where the birth actually took place is "worshipped" on the naming day, which is also the day that families of her community first put a baby in its cradle. A **castor oil** lamp is lit there, a **coconut** is broken, and two types of leaves are set on the place: *kakke soppu* (***Cassia fistula***) and *(y)ekkada(y)ele* (***Calotropis gigantea***).

Figure 1. A Winnowing Fan, the First Bed of a
Newborn Infant (photo of a miniature)

---

[16] This ritual procedure is meant to remove 'evil eye'.

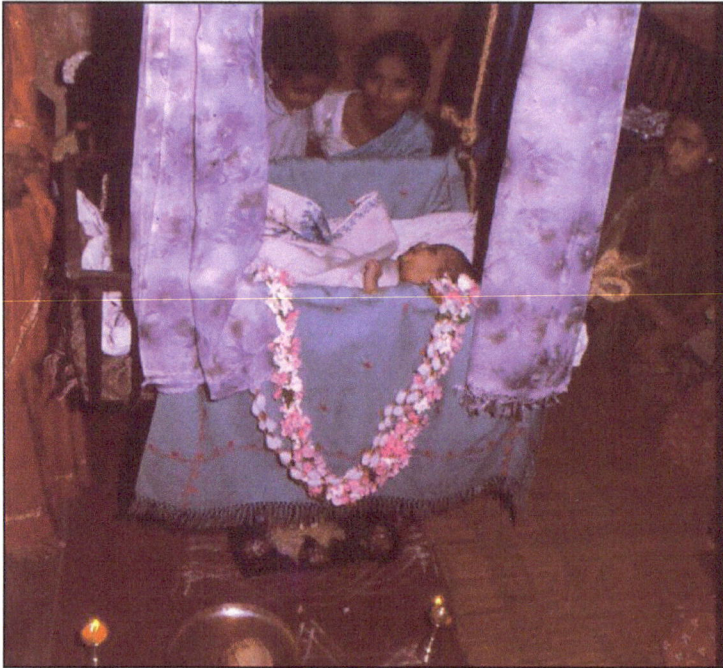

Figure 2. An Infant Just Moved to Its Cradle, with plantain leaf and rice set below it

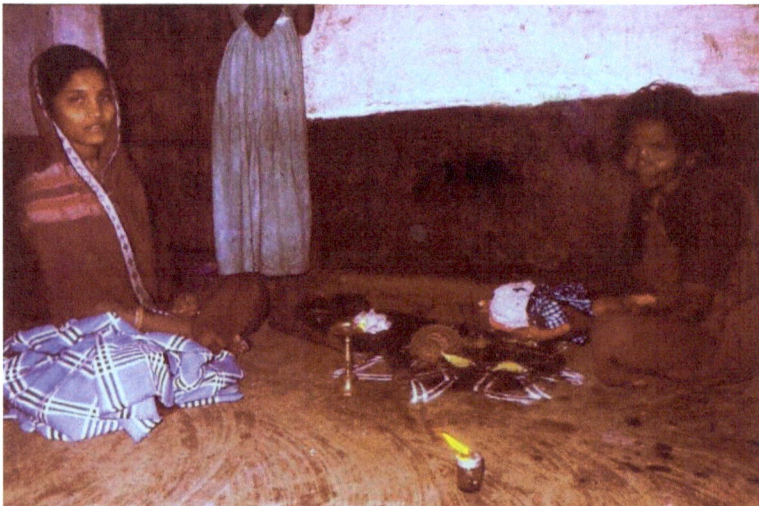

Figure 3. Offerings to the Place of a Birth, Scheduled Caste, Bandipur

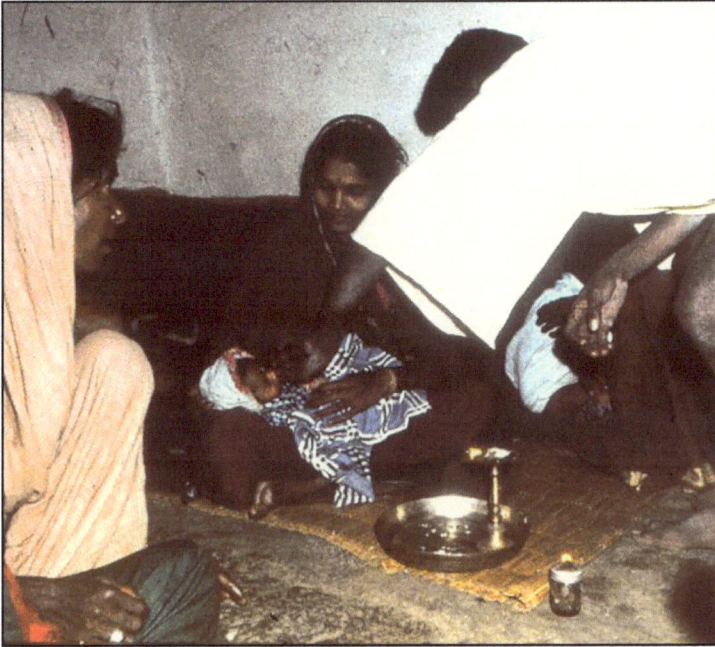

Figure 4. Putting *baj-beNNe* in the Mouth of a New Baby,
Scheduled Caste, Bandipur

Figure 5. A Typical *hase maNe* Wooden Platform

Naming rituals

According to the customs of most (but not all) castes, a baby is
formally named after the ten-day state of a family's birth-related 'ritual
pollution' (*sutaka*) is over.[17] On the 11th day after the birth, the house

17 We were told that the Fisherman caste custom is to name an infant three days after

is thoroughly cleaned and purified in preparation for the naming ceremony.[18] For non-Brahmans and Scheduled Caste families, this usually means white-washing the house and cleaning/purifying the floor with some cow dung and water. Clay pots are replaced with new ones, and metal pots are carefully cleaned[19]. The baby and mother bathe, as do other family members.

A priest of some sort (e.g., a *dasayya*, *aynoru*, or *purohit/joyish*) is usually called to help name the baby. This event is a festive one, so **a string of mango leaves** (*tooraNa*) will be hung over the front door; guests will be invited and fed a nice meal. The baby's father and other relatives (father's parents, paternal uncles, mother's parents, and so on) should be present on this occasion.

Beyond these common practices, naming rituals vary from one caste/subcaste to another. According to one Barber caste informant, the ritual specialist (an *aynoru* from a nearby town) comes to the house, sprinkles water in all parts of the house to purify it. He puts a holy mark, a *naama*, on the mother and baby and gives them a purifying drink called *tirtha*[20]. He then blesses all of those gathered and gives them *tirtha*; and they all prostrate to him. This Barber informant told us that, "The *Aynoru* selects a name, whispers it in the baby's ears, and all prostrate to him before he departs." He is paid with **raw rice**, some

---

its birth.

[18] As the first one or two children are generally born in the new mother's natal home, but sutaka applies to the patrilineal family, not this house, it seems likely that both houses might need purification, perhaps for different reasons.

[19] A Farmer caste villager, told us that, when using public wells, nobody will touch their water pitchers to those of a family whose lineage is in this state of ritual pollution. If the water pitchers do accidentally touch, they will be 'purified' with **tamarind**.

[20] This term is used for several types of of purifying or blessing liquids. Our notes in this case do not indicate what it actually is.

kind of *Daal,* **spices, vegetables** and some money; all of these items are presented to him in a winnowing fan (*moRa*). A Fisherman caste informant gave a similar description. In brief, the *Dasayya* priest removes the state of 'pollution' and then names the baby. The family does worship for their household God and offers food to the deity before eating the meal themselves. We heard a similar description from a Washerman caste informant, who said that the priest (*Aynoru*) prounces the name of the baby three times and puts the *naama* mark on it. In this community the baby is set into its cradle only after being named.

The priest is paid with a special mixture of things called *paDi*: raw rice, salt, pepper, jaggery, and flour made with finger millet (*hasiiTu*), coconut, betel-areca, and some money.

In one Farmer caste home we observed a local Brahman, serving as a priest (*purohit*), remove the *sutaka* pollution in the morning of the 11th day after a birth. He sprinkled the house with a *tiirtha* liquid (called *ganjala*, consisting of cow urine mixed with milk, honey, and yoghurt).[21] Some of this liquid was also given to the people gathered there to drink. In the evening of the same day, this priest returned to the house, and all "community members" (mostly caste-mates) were summoned. A small offering was made to the exact place where they baby had been born. Some white *rangoli* designs were painted on the floor there, and five sets of **plantains, betel leaves, and areca nuts** were set out – one each at four corners of the baby's winnowing fan bed, and one in the center. The priest chanted some mantras and said the baby's name was "MangaLa." All of those gathered came to the baby,

---

[21] This mixture's name means 'Ganga Water'. It is called *panchamrita*, or 'the five elixirs'. (Narayan Hegde, personal communication).

saying her name and putting a little "butter" [probably *baj-beNNe*] in her mouth. Their blessings were "good wishes for her whole life." After this a male relative waved the mixture of **rice paddy, finger millet, and horse gram** around the winnowing fan, as described earlier.

An informant from a different Farmer subcaste, the Daas Okkaligas, told us that their custom is for a priest (called *joyish*, probably a Brahman[22]) to come to the house carrying a small vessel full of water. He transforms this water into the purifying *tiirtha* by adding certain things to it, namely, cow urine, yoghurt, honey, jaggery, and *tuLasi* **leaves** (*Ocymum sanctum*). He sprinkles this liquid around the house with **mango leaves**. The priest then blesses the mother and baby, sprinkles *tiirtha* on the baby, and distributes it to those present. The priest then selects a name for the baby according to its birth time and astrological signs; and the baby is put at the feet of the priest. After this all others prostrate to the priest.

A woman of a different Farmer subcaste, the Mull Okkaligas, told us that the baby's maternal uncle (*sodaramaava*) would come to name the baby in consultation with a Brahman priest. The uncle speaks the name, and family members repeat it. He then ties a special thread (*uDudaara*) to the baby's waist, and married women put the **butter-nutmeg mixture** (*baj- beNNe*) into the baby's mouth.

Among Brahmans and the Smith (Achari) caste, the custom is to inscribe the baby's new name into a bed of **raw rice**. A Smith caste informant described the ceremony to us in this way:

---

[22] A *joyish* may be any type of priest. Priests who can make horoscopes would include Brahmans. (Helen Ullrich and Shalini R. Bhat, personal communication).

The new parents and baby are seated on special wooden platforms (*hase maNe*), the baby on its mother's lap. Those present 'put' **raw rice colored with turmeric powder** (the mixture called *akšate*) on the foreheads of the baby and its parents. Some **raw rice** is put onto a plate, and the baby's name is written into the rice. A **coconut** and one gold ring are set onto the plate. The priest (a Smith caste *joyish*) does a small worship (*puja*) for the plate and asks the parents to touch it. Then all the friends and relatives who are present also say the baby's name and touch the plate.

An Iyengar Brahman man explained that his caste's naming ceremony requires a whole turmeric rhizome:

The mother sits with the baby on her lap. According to their plans, the baby's father's family chooses a name, and they tell it to the priest (*purohit*). He writes the name on a plate of **raw rice** with a whole piece of **turmeric root** (*arasiNada-kombu*) and then does *puja* for the plate. After he says the name loudly three times, those present give gifts and bless the baby. A special mixture called *cherapu* is distributed to those present; it is made with **coconut, sugar, and betel nuts**. Food is then served to relatives and friends.

Foods brought to the birth house after one month

People of two castes (Fisherman and Scheduled Caste) – told us that approximately one month after a birth, the baby's father brings a collection of foods and other items (Kannada, *(y)ecca*) to the house where the baby was born, *i.e.,* his wife's natal home. Items carried on

23

this visit are called 'new mother flavors/spices' (*baaNanti kaara*) by the Scheduled Caste group. They include the following items: a sweet oil (*ucceLeNNe*), butter, 30 *seers* (30 kg.) of **raw rice**, garlic, cumin (*jiirige*), pepper, and 'other necessary things' [for cooking a meal]. A Fisherman caste father customarily brings a similar assortment of things: 60 *seers* of **raw rice**, butter, oil, thickened areca juice (*kaachu*), **cloves, nutmeg** (*jaayikaayi*), onions, a reddish material chewed with betel-areca (*patre*), and betel-areca sets. This community also calls this collection *baaNantikaara*.

Summary: Plants in Birth and Naming Rituals

To summarize this section, the ritually important plants found in birth, cradle, and naming ceremonies are listed in Table 1. While many of the plant items are widely used in folk rituals and others, Bengal gram (Kannada, *kaDale*) and nutmeg (*jaayikaayi*) are less well known 'puja things'. Inscribing a name into a bed of raw rice, customary among both the Smith and Iyengar Brahman groups, gives this all-important food grain the symbolic power to confirm or legitimize the naming process. The use of a whole turmeric root (*Curcuma longa*) by Brahmans as the "writing" implement lends a clear note of auspiciousness to the occasion.

The distinctive mixture of paddy, finger millet, and horse gram – the mixture called *accande* or *daanya* -- is another unique feature of cradle and naming rituals. Presented to the baby by its maternal uncle among the Daas Okkaliga subcaste of Farmers, and by the father among another group of Farmers, this same mixture is tied to a new baby's cradle by its mother in Scheduled Caste families.

Table 1. Plant Materials in Birth, Cradle, and Naming Rituals

Botanical Name [English]	Kannada Name	Uses (*widespread practice)
	Mixture *accande (or) daanya*	Finger millet, unhusked rice (paddy), and horse gram: required in cradle shaastra (*)
	Mixture *sunDal*	Combination of boiled or fried Bengal gram, salt, grated coconut, and seasonings, presented to married women participating in Iyengar cradle ceremony.
	(y)ecca	Combination of items for cooking a meal, brought to the new mother by her husband's family a month after a birth (*) -raw rice, oil, butter, onions, garlic, spices
Areca catechu [areca]	*aDike*	Areca nut paired with betel leaf, for distribution and for ritual set- up (cradle transition) (*)
	kaachu 'thickened areca juice'	Thickened areca juice included in foods brought to the birth house after one month, with *(y)ecca* (Fisherman)
Calotropis gigantea	*(y)ekka*	Leaf set together with *Cassia fistula* on place where birth occurred
Cassia fistula	*kakke*	Leaf set together with *Calotropis gigantea* on place where birth occurred

Table 1. Plant Materials in Birth, Cradle, and Naming Rituals

Botanical Name [English]	Kannada Name	Uses (*widespread practice)
Cicer arietinum [Bengal gram]	*kaDale*	-Soaked gram a prominent item in snacks distributed after cradle/naming rituals -Used in Iyengar cradle ritual: distributed to married women as part of the *sunDal* mixture.
Cocos nucifera [coconut]	*tengin kaayi* (whole coconut) *hombaaLe* (flower) *kobbari* (dried coconut)	whole coconut broken, after a birth, to avoid 'evil eye' (*) coconut flower (*hombaaLe*) crushed & mixed with milk, given as medicine to a new mother (Smartha custom) shredded, dried in *kaDale husli* preparation distributed in Iyengar cradle ritual
Curcuma longa [turmeric]	*arasiNa* -*kombu* (whole, not cut)	powdered, distributed with vermillion to married women; also used in worship of deities (*) whole rhizome, used to inscribe baby's name in a plate of raw rice
Eleusine coracana Gaertn [finger millet]	*raagi*	In *accande* mixture (*)
Macrotyloma uniflorum (Lam.) Verdc. [horse gram]	*huraLi kaaLu*	One part of the *accande* mixture, combined with finger millet and rice paddy(*)

Table 1. Plant Materials in Birth, Cradle, and Naming Rituals

Botanical Name [English]	Kannada Name	Uses (*widespread practice)
Mangifera indica [mango]	*maavu*	String of leaves hung on front door of house at end of 'pollution' period, before naming a baby (*) Leaf used to sprinkle water when purifying a house (*)
Musa sapientum [plantain]	*baaLe* -*haNNu* (ripe fruit) -*(y)ele* (leaf)	ripe fruit distributed to guests (*) leaf as setting for offering (*) Leaf put under cradle (Iyengar)
Myristica fragrans [nutmeg]	*jaayikaayi*	Mixture of nutmeg and butter, called *baj-beNNe*: put in mouth of baby making the transition to the cradle (*) Seasoning provided as part of Farmer caste *(y)ecca*.
Oryza sativa [rice]	*bhatta* (unhusked paddy) *akki* (uncooked)	In *accande* mixture (unhusked paddy) (*) Raw rice on plate where a baby's name is first written
Piper betle [betel]	*viLyad(y)ele*	Leaf paired with areca nut (*)
Ricinus communis [castor]	*haraLeNNe* (castor oil)	Oil used in lamp for worship for the place of birth
Saccharum spp. [sugar]	*bella* (unrefined/jaggery) *sakare* (refined sugar)	Jaggery kept in mouth of maternal uncle as he goes to the Maramma temple for a blessing (Farmer) Jaggery may be one ingredient in purifying *tirtha* liquid (Farmer house, Brahman priest). Refined sugar distributed after a birth

Botanical Name [English]	Kannada Name	Uses (*widespread practice)
Tamarindus indica [tamarind]	huNisehaNNu (fruit)	Considered to be a purifying substance: -Used to soak cloth holding *daanya* mixture, in Scheduled Caste cradle ritual -Used to purify water pots of non-family members, if they accidentally touch the water pots of family in a ritually polluted state

Maturation Rituals for Girls

During the period of our field research, families of all castes and sub-castes celebrated their girls' first menstrual periods in one way or another. We have details on the customs of three castes, plus some general information from three others; and we were able to observe two of these ceremonies.

Girls on this occasion were sometimes referred to as 'new mothers' (*baaNanti*), reflecting the fact that they could now become pregnant. In earlier days many would have been married as children and sent to live with their husbands' families after they matured. Child marriage, however, was no longer practiced in these two villages in the 1960s, and all teenage girls went to school.

A girl's first menstruation supposedly creates a state of ritual 'pollution' for her patrilineal group. However, we were told different things by different caste informants about how long it lasts and to whom it applies. All agreed that the girl herself was 'unclean' (*mailige*) while menstruating, as all women were (are) considered to be. Some people on this occasion used the same term for family pollution

28

(*sutaka*) as that used for occasions of birth and death. The head of the Scheduled Caste community of Bandipur Village told our assistant, K. Gurulingaiah, for example, that for one month the girl herself was "*sutaka*," as was the whole patrilineal group. No others would accept food or water from them during this month. In this community the houses were purified in the same ways that they were when the birth 'pollution' period was over. A Farmer caste family also told us that a girl's first menstruation creates a condition of *sutaka* for one month for the whole patrilineal family.[23]

Other comments seemed to limit the ritual 'pollution' state to the girl herself, and to observe restrictions for variable amounts of time. A Smartha Brahman neighbor, for example, told me that a newly menstruating girl is 'polluted' for three months, after which she must take a river bath to become pure. This same neighbor said that girls in earlier times (but not now) were kept in the house for this three month period and fed special, delicious foods, mostly ones considered 'heating'. She did not mention a 'polluting' state affecting the whole patrilineage. One Smith caste man told us that a newly mature girl was kept 'out of the kitchen' (the most carefully guarded part of a house) for five days after her first menstrual period, and that all 'pollution' disappeared after she was bathed and celebrated with suitable rituals. A Fisherman caste woman told us that after only two days of sitting apart from others, the girl bathed, and that was the end of it.

A girl's mother's family, especially her mother's brother (*sodarmaava*) is an especially important participant in this ritual. This is clearly related to the fact that in the South Indian (or Dravidian)

---

[23] I observed one situation, however, in which a Farmer caste girl's first menstruation came at an inconvenient time, when a family was celebrating a marriage; and it was kept secret until a little later, so that the grand occasion could go on.

marriage system the children of a sister and brother are considered especially suitable as marriage partners. The mother's brother also is considered to be a possible husband. Some lyrics of a song[24] sung at a Farmer caste (Okkaliga) ceremony on this occasion emphasize this special relationship:

> She is going out the door, to sit 'outside'. Tell her mother's people, her mother's brother, the news. Tell it to her mother's elder brother, and he will be happy. **He will bring jasmine leaves** to the girl. **He will take the flowers off of the plants and string them into a garland to put over her head...** Now tell the mother's younger brother. He smiles. He too brings jasmine leaves and takes flowers off of the plants to make a garland for her..When the girl has matured, her friends stand next to her out on the street. Rain comes on them, so her father has **a 'flower tent'** (*huuvin guDaara*) built for her. (1976 field notes)

The branches (referred to as either *kone* or *soppu*) of certain **trees** are very important on this occasion. Among non-Brahmans and Scheduled Caste families,[25] at least, the newly menstruating girl sits inside a shed (*guDisalu/guDlu*) built from branches of three specific trees: **country fig, jackfruit, and mango.** Earlier practice, as documented by Bhattacharyya (1995:20ff.) and others, probably was for the girl to sit outside the house, or perhaps even outside the village, in a specially built hut. But by the mid-20th century, her temporary

---

[24] This is a sample of a genre of songs, Sobbhana Songs, sung on this occasion.

[25] We have detailed information only from Farmer (Okkaliga), Fisherman (Bestaru), and Scheduled Caste (A.K.) informants on this practice, but it was known to be widespread in the region at the time of this research. Brahmans and Smith (Achari) families, however, did not seem to do this.

leaf shed was set in the house near the front door, in the section referred to as the 'outside', that is, completely separated from the kitchen and the shrine to the family's house god, which are referred to as the 'inside' of the house. According to one Scheduled Caste informant, her mother's brother (*sodaramaava*) builds the leaf shed. In the Farmer caste, a boy of a 'separate house' – probably a cousin or an uncle eligible to be her husband -- builds it. Before she sits inside the leaf shed, he and the girl playfully splash each other with water, and he breaks a **coconut**, which he is required to take away to his own house afterwards. (Figure 7)

Once the girl is seated inside her leaf shed on a *hase maNe*, the family does a ritual for her. It is called 'lap filling' (*maDilu-tumbu*) – a term referring to the front of her sari (*maDilu*), which covers her lap as she sits. Some customary items are required for this: in Fisherman caste homes, **raw rice, coconut, jaggery cubes, and ripe plantains**. The Scheduled Caste family makes a slightly different presentation, doing so before she goes into her leaf shed: **ripe plantains, coconut, betel-areca set, puffed rice (*puri*), and Bengal gram**. After doing the 'lap-filling', it is the custom of this caste for three married women to 'put' rice on the girl: taking hands full of **raw rice**, the women put their hands on her knees and her shoulders three times each; then all three together throw rice on top of her head.

In one Farmer caste home we were told that items for the girl's 'lap-filling' are almost the same as those for a bride on the day before her wedding, but <u>without</u> one thing that only a bride gets, namely, an areca flower. The things offered to the newly menstruating girl are: two small packets *(kaT)* of **betel leaves**, five **dried coconuts** (*kobbari*), five large balls of the preparation called *tambiTTu*, which is made with

Bengal gram and **sesame seeds**, some ripe **plantains**, two **coconuts**, and three or five pieces of the 'heating' snack called *chigaNivunde*, which is made with **jaggery**, black **sesame seeds**, and **cardamom**.

Another song that we heard sung by one Farmer family for a girl in her leaf shed compares the girl to happy, growing plants. It is called the 'Putting Rice' song, because they sing it while putting rice on her. Some of the lyrics are as follow:

> At the Tuppagiri Mallayya Mountain Temple there is a plantain garden. Our girl's life should be good like that... **Banana flowers and growing, unripe banana fruit (***baaLekaayi***),** as you are happy, so our girl should be happy. **Coconuts and coconut trees,** as you are happy, so our girl should be happy. .. As the parrots fly over Baguru, drop mustard seeds on our girl. [My assistant, a member of this family, explains: the word for mustard seeds is used here because of its sound. The true reference is dropping **raw rice** on the girl.] (1976 field notes)

According to one Smith caste (Achari) family we interviewed, the newly matured girl has an oil bath five days after her first menstrual period; and she is celebrated by married women as she sits on the small wooden platform. The married women sing to her and offer their blessings. Turmeric-vermillion, flowers, ripe plantains, and sugar are distributed to those gathered for the occasion. There was no mention of her sitting under a leaf shed.

Figure 7. Maternal Uncle of Farmer Caste Girl Coming out of Her Leaf Shed (Bandipur, 1967

Figure 6. Farmer Caste Girl in Her Leaf Shed

Figure 8. Lap-filling Ceremony for a Scheduled Caste Girl (Bandipur)

An important presentation to a girl in Farmer caste families is called *(y)ecca*. This word comes up in wedding ceremonies, as a

33

collection of edible items and other gifts carried between the bride's and groom's houses. On this occasion a basket is prepared for the girl by the people of a different house, one that is connected to hers by marriage: people called *neNTru*.[26] The basket is filled with the following items: two bunches *(chippu)* of **ripe plantains**; a combined total of 12 **coconuts** and **dried coconuts**; four squares *(achu)* of **jaggery**; two tied bundles *(kaT)* of **betel leaves**; one-quarter kg. (one *pow*) of **areca nuts**; two kg. (two *seers*) of butter ('for the *baaNanti*/new mother to eat'); some **nutmeg** because it is 'cooling'; a reddish material chewed with betel-areca *(patre)*; some thickened areca juice *(kaachu)*; flowers; a blouse piece; and a sari.

Families of some castes may do further rituals a month or more after the girl's initial ceremonies. One Smartha Brahman family told me, for example, that a girl must go for a river bath three months after her first menstrual period, in order to be considered 'pure' again. This same family mentioned an old custom, no longer observed, in which the second menstrual period of a girl was celebrated with the preparation and serving of two kinds of the popular, steamed snack called *kaDabu*, presented to her with other things in a special 'wealth-wishing' *(bhaagina)* container.

A Scheduled Caste informant in Bandipur Village told us that one month after a girl's first menstrual period the whole house is cleaned, the floor being smeared with cow dung and some cow urine. All clay pots are replaced with new ones, and metal pots are purified with **tamarind**. A priest (Daasayya) is invited to the house to worship the family deity and blow a conch shell horn after food has been cooked

---

[26] My notes do not indicate at which stage of the girl's ritual this presentation is made.

and offered (the offering is called *(y)eDe*) to God. After the meal has been served and eaten, the girl is set on a wooden platform (*hase maNe*), and the family does the 'lap-filling' ceremony for her. After this she is considered to be 'pure' (*maDi*).

In Chinnapura Village we observed the procession of a Scheduled Caste family with musical accompaniment, announcing and celebrating the passage of six weeks since their girl's first menstrual period. They were carrying the collection of food items called *(y)ecca*, in this case consisting of the following items: **dried coconut, jaggery, Bengal gram, betel-areca, sesame, butter, and ripe plantains.** This party was led by the girl's mother's father, her mother's brother, her mother's sister's husband, and five married women. Stanley Regelson's notes quote a participant saying that, "These are the same people who would bring *(y)ecca* to a new mother (*baaNanti*)." Fifteen men danced joyfully well into the night after this procession.

This same family brought their girl to the river the next morning to worship Ganga, the river goddess. Setting three vessels of water (*kaLashas*) and some mud images under a turmeric- colored cloth, they sprinkled on them **'five kinds of grain'** (*daanya*): **sorghum, finger millet, unhusked rice, sesame,** and *tadguni/halsande* (*Vigna catjang,* a type of bean). The girl had some butter on her hair; her mother's brother had put it there on the preceding evening and again in the morning. After the worship for Ganga, a group of women sang songs praising the goddess's 'thin lips and narrow face'. At the conclusion of this event, the girl broke a **coconut** and two women of her patrilineage did some kind of ceremony (shaastra) for her. We were told that, 'It is compulsory that half of this coconut should go to the musicians'.

Summary: Plants in Girl's Maturation Rituals

To summarize the ethnobotany aspect of this section, some items are the same as in birth and naming rituals: especially ripe coconuts, ripe plantains, and betel-areca sets. Nutmeg also was mentioned briefly, as one of the items for *(y)ecca* in the Farmer caste ritual; and Bengal gram appears as a separate item, and as an ingredient in a required snack. But there are some prominent new botanicals here, especially the three types of **tree branches** used to build the girl's leaf shed. **Betel leaves**, not just betel-areca sets, also figure prominently in the Farmer caste affines'[27] presentation (*(y)ecca*) to the girl.

Breaking a ripe coconut once again is used to fend off spiritual danger. Ritual participants explained to us that half of the broken coconut absolutely must <u>not</u> remain with the girl or her household. In the Bandipur Farmer caste interviews, the boy who builds the leaf shed, who lives elsewhere, is required to take away half of the coconut that is broken during the set-up. In the Chinnapura Scheduled Caste ceremony at the river we observed six weeks after their girl's first menstruation, participants told us that the family is strictly required to give half of their broken coconut to the musicians who accompanied them on their procession.

Dry coconuts (*kobbari*) appear here in the 'lap-filling' ritual of the Farmer caste and in *(y)ecca* offerings by members of the Scheduled Caste. One Scheduled Caste family was observed to use **tender coconuts** (*siyaaLi*) in their 'lap-filling' ritual.

Table 2 lists the more important specific plants required for these rituals. And Table 3 summarizes information on the special **mixtures**

---

[27] Affines are kin groups related by marriage, rather than by descent.

of plants and food items required for 'lap-filling' and other maturation ceremonies of three different castes.

Table 2. Uses of Specific Plants in Girls' Maturation Rituals

Botanical Name [English]	Kannada Name	Uses (*widespread practice)
Artocarpus heterophyllus Lam. (family, Moraceae /Artocarpaceae) [jackfruit]	*haLasina - mara* 'tree' *-kone or soppu* 'leafy branch'	Required for leaf shed for newly menstruating girl(*)
Cicer arietinum [Bengal gram]	*kaDale*	Ingredient in cooked preparation, Farmer caste 'lap-filling' ritual; Item required for Scheduled Caste 'lap-filling' ritual.
Cocos nucifera [coconut]	*kobbari* [dry, without shell] *siyaaLi* 'tender coconut' *tenginkaayi* 'ripe coconut'	Used in lap-filling ritual(*) Part of *(y)ecca* food presentations. Used in river ritual six weeks after the girl's first menstruation (Scheduled Caste)
Ficus glomerata Roxb. (family, Moraceae) [country fig]	*attimara tree* *-kone or soppu* leafy branch	Required for leaf shed for newly menstruating girl(*)
Mangifera indica L. (family, Anacardiaceae) [mango]	*maavinmara* 'tree' *-kone or soppu* 'leafy branch'	Required for leaf shed for newly menstruating girl(*)
Myristica fragrans [nutmeg]	*jaaikaayi*	One item in the basket of things presented as *(y)ecca* to the girl by her family's affines (*neNTru*)

Table 2. Uses of Specific Plants in Girls' Maturation Rituals

Botanical Name [English]	Kannada Name	Uses (*widespread practice)
Oryza sativa [rice]	akki (uncooked, raw rice)	Raw rice: set onto the girl's knees, shoulders, and head in the 'putting' ritual.
	puri (puffed)	Puffed rice is used in the 'lap-filling' ritual (Scheduled Caste)
	bhatta (unhusked rice)	Unhusked rice used in 30-day ritual (Scheduled Caste)
Piper betle [betel]	viLyadele (betel leaf)	Two kaT of leaves in the basket of things presented as (y)ecca to the girl by her family's affines (neNTru) (Farmer caste)
Sorghum bicolor [sorghum]	jooLa	Used in Scheduled Caste 30-day ritual
Tamarindus indica L. (family, Caesalpiniaceae /Leguminosae) [tamarind]	huNise	Used to purify metal pots at end of 'pollution' period (Scheduled Caste)
Others: areca nuts, ripe plantains, jaggery, flowers		Items in 'lap-filling' rituals, and/or in basket of (y)ecca

Table 3. Named Combinations of Plant Items in Girls'
Maturation Rituals

Kannada Term	Caste or Sub-caste Customs		
	Fisherman (Bestaru)	Farmer (Okkaliga)	Scheduled Caste (A.K.)
maDilutumbu 'lap- filling' shaastra	Raw rice, ripe plantains, fresh coconut, jaggery cubes	Ripe plantains, fresh coconuts, dry coconuts, betel leaves, snacks made with Bengal gram (*tambiTTu*), & sweet balls made with sesame and jaggery (*ciganivunde*)	Ripe plantains, Bengal gram, tender coconuts, betel-areca combination
(y)ecca presented in a basket by affines	No information	Ripe plantains, fresh coconuts, dry coconuts, betel leaves, areca nuts, jaggery, butter, nutmeg, *patre, kachu,* flowers	Ripe plantains, dry coconuts, jaggery, Bengal gram, Sesame, butter, and betel-areca
daanya-daavsa 'grains, grams, and pulses'	No information	No information	'Five kinds of *daanya*' in ritual at the river, 30 days after first menstruation: sorghum (*jooLa*), finger millet (*raagi*), unhusked rice (*bhatta*), sesame (*puT(y)eLLu,* and *tadguni/halsande* (*Vigna catjang,* a bean)

Initiation Rituals for Boys

Unlike girls', ritual celebration of boys' maturation is not universal among all castes. We found two different kinds of boy's initiation rites in the villages where we did our fieldwork. (1) Among non-Brahmans and the Scheduled Caste (A.K./Holeya), ceremonies for maturing boys are customary only among those families who have joined the Vaishnavite *Daas* sect, which is dedicated to the God at Thirupathi. This multi-caste group designates some of its sons (usually the eldest) as religious mendicants who live on the charity of others and serve as priests.[28] One Farmer caste informant told us that their custom is to do it for only the eldest and youngest sons. This community calls the ritual *deevarige mudre biDuvudu*, meaning 'putting on the mark of God'. After he has gone through this ritual, a boy is considered a *Daasayya*. (2) Brahmans and Smith castes conduct a ceremony for all boys or young men when they first put on the "sacred thread," or *jenevaara*. This occasion is called *munji* or *upanayana*.

Again unlike girls, boys do not have a fixed age at which they go through these ritual initiations. One Iyengar Brahman explained to us, for example, that the *munji* or *upanayana* ceremony could be done "any time after a boy reaches age seven, up to age 24. But it must be done before his marriage." Smartha Brahmans told us that the ceremony could be done any time after a boy is eight years old; and a Smith caste informant said it is done after a boy completes 11 years of age. Among Daas families of the Farmer, Washerman, and Barber castes, a boy's

---

[28] Nanjundayya, H.V., and Rao Bahadur L.K. Ananthakrishna Iyer, 1930, *The Mysore Tribes and Castes*. Mysore: Mysore University Press, vol III, pp. 101-115.

ceremony is done between the time he reaches age 15 and his marriage[29]. (Some do it on the day before the wedding.)

The Sanskritic referent of these rituals is, of course, the boy's entry into the stage of life called *brahmacharya*, the celibate-student phase during which he depends on charity to survive. So some kind of local 'begging' is part of all these initiation ceremonies.

Although a priest officiates, Brahman rituals give special focus to the boy's connection with his parents, who sit with him for much of the time. The boy's transition to a different stage of life is signified by his eating together (from the same leaf-plate) with his mother for the last time in his life, according to an Iyengar Brahman custom[30]. The father's role is more as a teacher or, in some families, a "guru" who explains special mantras to the boy.

While this event represents a significant transition in a family's life cycle, it does not create the ritual pollution state that birth and girls' ceremonies do. Nonetheless, details from some of our interviews mention the same careful purification procedures being followed as on those other occasions. One Farmer caste report, for example, says that, "The house is whitewashed and smeared with cow dung. All utensils are cleaned, and clay pots are all replaced with new ones. And all family members take a bath." A Smartha Brahman explained to us that a special ceremony, *naandi shaastra*, is done to "remove all pollution." An Iyengar Brahman and a Smith caste informant both said it was

---

[29] Some Scheduled Caste families identify themselves as Daas and do rituals for boys; but we do not have detailed information on their rituals.

[30] A verbal report from an Iyengar Brahman said that the boy eats sitting next to his mother but from a different leaf-plate. The report above, however, is based on an Iyengar ritual that we observed.

important for the boy and his parents to bathe and put on 'pure' (*maDi*) clothes before the ceremony.

Like the ceremonies for girls, boys' initiation rites involve many plant materials, including sticks or twigs of some specific trees. In the boys' initiation rites, the sacred fig tree is especially important among all castes for whom we have information.

Non-Brahman Daasayya Initiation Rituals

Among the non-vegetarian castes, it is customary to butcher a male goat or ram for the feast that will follow the ceremony. Farmer, Washerman, and Barber boys are initiated in a ritual at the river after cooking has started. They go there accompanied by priests and musicians. Someone in the group is holding an oil torch (*panju*). And certain items required for the ceremony at the river are carried along:

> Farmers' (Okkaliga) river ritual - The group carries with them to the river a small water pot with an **areca/coconut flower**[31] in it (*hombaaLe kaLasha*), some plantains, coconuts, soaked, sweetened raw **rice** (*nene akki*), turmeric and vermillion, some **jackfruit** pieces (*haLasina tooLe*), and four 'cane sticks' *(bettada koolu)*—made from **tender bamboo**. Also small, wooden images of deities, often worn while dancing: *baNanta deevaru & kariyaNNa halage*.

> At the river a washed cloth is spread over these offerings. The four cane sticks are bundled up (into a *bilguD*) with a red towel.

---

[31] Our notes mention *hombaaLe*, not specifying whether it is an areca or a coconut flower. But I assume that it is an areca flower, because the coconut flower has inauspicious connotations.

Some *kakke* flowers (*Cassia fistula*) are tied onto the bundle. A priest does worship for five small vessels of water, each with four- *anna* coins inside and a **coconut** on top. These vessels are adorned with **mango leaves**, flowers, and turmeric-vermillion.

He then puts a metal bracelet (*kapaDa*) on the boy's right hand, and the *naama* blessing- sign on him and all the others who are present. He teaches some mantras to the boy after giving him three items: *shanku, jaagaTe, and jooLige.*[32] The boy is now a *daasayya*.

<u>Washerman caste river ritual</u> - The boy goes to the river with an umbrella carried over his head and an oil torch bearer nearby. With him are musicians, an *Aynoru* priest, and a *daasayya*. The group is carrying images of Hanuman and three other deities (Baamamta deevaru, Kenearaayana harige, and Koriraayana harige) and items needed for the ritual: one **cane stick** (tender **bamboo**), **flowers, coconuts, jackfruit** pieces, flowers, and *Cassia fistula* leaves (Kannada, *kakke*).

At the river they keep the things together and "make a *bilguD*." The icons are worshipped, and a silver *kappaDa* (bracelet) is put on the boy, along with *šanku, jaagaTe*, and *joLige*. A leafy branch of **Cassia fistula** and the **cane stick** are placed in his hand. The Aynoru puts *naama* on him and then "scratches his tongue and right shoulder" with a **stick of neem** (*Azidrachta*

---

[32] The *shanku* a wooden post or stick of some sort; *jaagaTe* is a circular metal plate or gong 'used by religious mendicants'; and *jooLige* is 'a square piece of cloth gathered up at the edges, into which alms are put', according to *Kittel's KannaDa-English Dictionary*.

indica) while chanting "Govinda" and mantras. From that time onward, the boy is a *daasayya*.

<u>Barber (Hajamru) caste river ritual</u> – The boy walks to the river under a large umbrella and is accompanied by a *daasayya* priest and musicians ("pipe and drum"), and an oil torch bearer. Items carried by the group are: deities (Hanuman, *baaNanta deevaru*, and *kencharayara harige*), one **cane stick, plantains, coconuts, and jackfruit** pieces.

At the river they 'perform *bilguD*'[33] and worship the deities. After the *puja*, the priest puts a silver *kappaDa* on the boy. He puts in the boy's hand the following items: *šanku, jaagaTe, joLige, kakke* **leaves**, and the **cane stick.** He puts a *naama* on the boy and then "scratches his tongue and right shoulder" with a **stick from a neem tree** while chanting mantras, repeating "Govinda" many times. The boy now has the status of *daasayya*.

On the way back to the house, the group places a long cloth (*maNevu*) with jaggery sprinkled on it at many spots along the way. The boy walks on this[34]. Images of the deities are installed in the home shrine, and food (*(y)eDe)* is offered to them. After this worship, the family has food with friends and relatives.

There are so many common features in these three descriptions, that we can safely assume that they represent a general non-Brahman

---

[33] Notes do not specify the meaning of this.
[34] Mr. Malla Setty has provided me with the meanings of many of the terms used.

approach to a Daas boy's initiation, and probably also that of the Daas families of the Scheduled Caste who do this ritual.

On the evening after the boy becomes a *daasayya*, there is a joyful celebration, with general feasting and worship of family deities, to whom food also is offered. The next morning, among the Farmer caste, the house is purified and the boy puts on clean clothes. Then the boy goes out "begging" together with another, older *daasayya*. Neighbors give him food items, which his family will cook when he returns home. (We do not have information on whether the Washermen and Barber boys go out "begging" or not, but it is likely that they do.)

That same day, the day after the boy has become a *daasayya*, Barbers and Farmers perform a **marriage ceremony between the boy and a sacred fig tree.**[35] The Barber caste custom is for the boy to go to the tree with the *Aynoru* priest and musicians. Some auspicious, wedding-type items are set at the base of the tree: a small vessel of water (*kaLasha*), a mirror, some turmeric and vermillion, and some flowers. The priest(s) tie a **turmeric rhizome** with a string (a *kankaNa*) onto the boy's wrist as he sits on a wooden platform next to the tree. Married women pay homage to him, and the priest chants some mantras. Then the boy ties the marital pendant, a *taaLi*, onto the tree. From this day on, our informant told us, "the boy has higher status in society. He will be treated as equal with married men."

For the Farmer caste **tree-marriage ceremony,** the group also brings with them a vessel (*kaLasha*), a small mirror, turmeric and vermillion, plus some festive turmeric-colored **raw rice** (*akshate*), betel-

---

[35] Our notes do not indicate whether the Washermen did this ritual or not, but it seems likely that they did.

areca sets, plantains, and coconuts. The Farmer boy also wears the **turmeric rhizome** tied by a thread on his wrist. He "ties a thread [a marital *taaLi*] to the tree," and the priest performs the ceremony called *dhaare* uniting them in marriage. After the marriage, his turmeric rhizome *kankaNa* is removed[36]. Some married women offer blessings to the boy and to the tree, and all return home. Food cooked from his "begged" items is offered in worship to the gods, and the boy blows a conch-shell horn and a bugle. Other *daasayyas* give food to him, further confirming his new, higher status.

Brahman and Smith Caste Sacred Thread Ceremonies

We have information on boys' initiation rituals as done by three other castes: Iyengar Brahmans, Smartha Brahmans, and the Smith (Achari) caste. They conduct their boys' initiation rites very differently from those just described, including more classical elements, such as a fire ceremony (*homa*); and they all mark the boy's transition by putting a "sacred thread" (*janivaara*) on him. Nonetheless, these ceremonies, different as they are, also require much plant material, especially twigs, sticks, and leafy branches, to get a boy to the next stage of life.

In preparation for their boy's ritual, a family builds a **leaf-covered** *pandal* in front of their house.[37] The boy and his parents bathe and put on new clothes (the boy has an oil bath). The hair on the front of the boy's head is shaved by a member of the Barber caste, who is paid in food items[38] as well as some money. (Figure 9) Among the Smartha

---

[36] The notes are not clear on why this is done, or what happens to the *kankaNa*.

[37] Brahman and Smith caste reports.

[38] Raw rice, jaggery, tur Daal (*togari beeLe*), spice power, salt, some tamarind, a snack to fry, called *happaLa (papadum)*; and some cooking oil (Smith caste report)

Brahmans, the boy wears a "false *janivaara*" while he is being shaved. His father puts on a "real" one on him later, as the boy takes the vows of the *brahmacharya*. While taking his vows, he holds a branch (*danDakoolu*) of **bastard teak** (*Butesa monosperma*) in his hand. The next day, the boy takes another oil bath, and there are further ceremonies for him. In the evening he carries a branch of **bastard teak** as he goes in procession around the village. After this he and his entourage all go to the **sacred fig tree** at the entrance to the village. He circles the tree three times and then carefully inserts his branches into the sacred fig, "so the wind cannot blow them off the tree." The family distributes a small treat to those who have gathered: some **Bengal gram,** *kosambri* salad,[39] and a mixture of jaggery and water called *panaka.*

The **bastard teak** branch or stick also is used in the Iyengar Brahman boy's *upanayana/munji* initiation ceremony. The sequence of events on the *upanayana/munji* day includes the following activities:

- The boy and his parents, all bathed and wearing clean clothes, sit together on a wood platform in front of a small silver vessel full of water (a *kaLasha*), with betel leaves and one coconut covering its mouth. It is set on a **plantain leaf** that is covered with **raw rice**. The boy's father sprinkles water with a **mango leaf** on the vessel, and it is carried to the household shrine for presentation to the family's household deity. The raw rice is given to the priest.

- *Godumkal shaastra* – Five married women sing songs as they grind some *suji* (coarsely ground rice) with a grinding stone

---

[39] Made with grated cucumber, coconut, green gram or other Daal, and spices.

that has set around it a symmetrical arrangement of four sets of soaked **Bengal gram** and **jaggery** on top of **betel leaves**. Each has an image of Ganesh, in the form of a cow dung mound with some **Cynodon dactylon** (*garike*) grass stuck into each mound. After this they pound some **turmeric** into powder while still singing. **Areca nuts**, turmeric-vermillion, and soaked **Bengal gram** are then distributed to the married women. The Brahman priests who helped with the initial ritual are given some food.

- The hair on the front of the boy's head is shaved off, in a semi-circular shape.

- *darbha shaastra* – The boy and his parents are seated on the wooden platform, the boy wearing a **turmeric-colored cloth** dhoti. The priest ties some *Poa cynosuroides, or "darbha* grass" around the waist of the boy, like a thread. Next, the boy puts on his sacred thread, *janivaara*.

- *chaolakanti uuTa* – Food is served to the boy and his mother on one plantain leaf. (The father does not eat at this time.) They eat their food, and everyone understands that this is the last time they will sit and eat together in this way.[40]

---

[40] We observed this event directly. A verbal report from a different Iyengar Brahman family said that the boy was to eat from a separate leaf but sitting next to his mother, meaning "together" with her. This source said that he would not sit and eat in the same line with his mother after that.

- A boy who has already undergone the initiation rite hands a branch of **bastard teak** to the initiate. This is called *danDin koolu koDuvudu*, or 'giving the *danDin* branch'.

- The boy prostrates to his mother three times, and she puts some offerings into a silver cup he holds: three handfuls of **raw rice**, one pearl, one piece of **jaggery**, and some **areca nuts**. Then his sisters give him "alms" on a plate: two fried snacks (*chakkali*), two sweet snacks made with sesame and jaggery (*ciganivunde/yeLLunde*), two **plantains**, one **coconut**, and some **areca nuts**. Other Brahman women also give him "alms."[41] These offerings are all given to the priest.[42]

- *Sabha puja* - Relatives of the boy give him gifts of things and money. Only "blood relatives" (*rakta sambandigaLu*) give, not others.

- Food is served to friends and relatives.

- (Observation, Bandipur Village) The boy goes in a procession with another, already initiated, to the **sacred fig tree** at the entrance to the village. Both have small branches of **bastard teak** tucked into their clothes. (Verbal description:) He walks around the tree three times, and does worship for the tree. (Observation, Bandipur Village:) A branch of the **bastard teak** is set into a notch in the trunk of

---

[41] Only women make these offerings, not men.

[42] This is an abbreviated account of an important and widespread practice in Brahman initiations: the newly initiated boy begs for alms, reciting in Sanskrit, *"Bhavati bhikshandehi,"* meaning that as a *brahmachari* he will be living henceforth only on alms. (Narayan Hegde, personal communication)

the tree. (Verbal description:) Married women circle a plate of red liquid in front of him in the rite called *aarati*, to remove the 'evil eye'.

- (Observation, Chinnapura Village) After doing worship at the tree, the group went to the village temple. When they returned to the family house, the boy's grandfather (father's father) threw a coconut down onto the steps, smashing it into pieces, and village children rushed to pick them up.

The Iyengar Brahman man who told us all this said that in his youth the ceremony took a long time, three days, but nowadays it is completed in one day. The custom was to keep a fire going in a clay pot for three days, using a kind of slow-burning wood as fuel. The boy, dressed in turmeric-colored cloth, did worship for the fire while sitting on a *hase maNe* (wooden platform). On the fourth day he took a branch of **bastard teak** from a boy who had already undergone the initiation and went in procession to the **sacred fig tree**, where he offered worship to the tree. After returning home, married women did *aarati* for him and sang special songs. The women were given a mixture of **dry coconut and sugar,** together with some areca nuts and flowers.

The Smith caste ceremony proceeds as follows:

- The boy and his parents sit on a wooden platform, and married women rub a mixture of **turmeric** and oil onto all of their cheeks. They get up, and the floor space where they sat is rubbed with cow dung, to purify it. A special design (*rangoli*) is drawn over that space, and the wooden platform is set back onto it.

50

- The boy sits on the wooden platform, and a Barber shaves the front of his head after doing worship for his own instruments. The Barber is paid with money and some food items.[43] After being shaved, the boy takes a bath and puts on a new dhoti and towel, which have been dipped in **turmeric-**colored water. The parents also put on new clothes

- The boy and his parents sit again on the wooden platform for another ritual, called *navagraha puja*. After this they do a 'fire worship' (*homada puja*) with **nine kinds of sticks** (*kaDDi*).[44] The boy's parents take the sticks, one-by-one, dipping each one in clarified butter and putting it into the fire.

- The priest takes one of the sticks, dips it into the clarified butter, and holds it in the fire. The boy puts out his tongue and the priest burns it slightly, thus "removing the defilement that ever came from eating the food of other castes."

- Next, the priests puts the *janivaara* onto the boy and teaches him the Gayitri Japa and other mantras.

---

[43] Four *annas* as *dakshiNe* (money payment), one coconut, betel-areca, plantains, one kg. (*seer*) of rice, jaggery, some *Daal*, spice powder, salt, tamarind, *happaLa/papadum* to fry, and some cooking oil.

[44] Sacred fig, bastard teak, *Achyranthes aspera* (Kannada, *uttaraNikaDDi*), *bannikaDDi* (some type of palm), *Calotropis gigantea* (Kannada, *(y)ekkadakaDDi)*, country fig (Kannada, *hatti/atti-kaDDi*), banyan (Kannada, *haalada/aalada-kaDDi*), *Poa cynosuroides* (Kannada, *darbhe,* a grass), and *toreenukaDDi* (no i.d. available).

- The boy goes around the room "begging" for alms: those present give him coins, which he gives to the priest. He then sits down on the wooden platform, and the priest blesses him. He receives gifts from the relatives and friends who are present.

- The boy then goes to the village **sacred fig tree**, where he does worship for God and others do *aarati* for him. All return to the house, where food is served to guests.

- In the evening after food women and children celebrate the boy. Married women sing songs for him and put vermillion on his forehead. The women are given turmeric- vermillion and some flowers; girls get some plantains and areca nuts, and boys get **Bengal gram flour.**

Summary

Table 4 summarizes our information on plant materials used in these two types of initiation rituals for boys. Certain plants are prominent. Among the Farmers, Barbers, and Washermen they are **jackfruit** (inner fruit pieces, not the large whole fruits seen on trees), **bamboo** 'cane sticks', *Cassia fistula* (Kannada *kakke*) in the river ritual; the **neem** (Kannada *beevinmara*) in the Barber caste rite; and the **sacred fig tree** (Farmers and Barbers). Among Brahmans and Smith castes the **sacred fig** also figures prominently, though without the marriage rite; and the other plant of special importance is the **bastard teak.** The Smith caste custom of using nine types of sticks, dipped in clarified butter, to fuel the sacred fire and burn the initiate's tongue is also noteworthy. In these rituals the sticks, branches, and trees are given symbolic responsibilities as witnesses and partners in a growing boy's spiritual development.

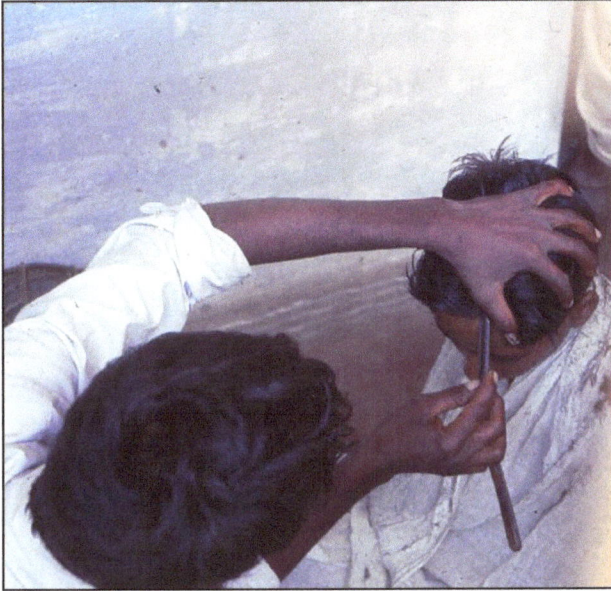

Figure 9. Brahman Boy Getting a Shave from a Local Barber (Bandipur Village, 1967)

Figure 10. Brahman Boy with His Father and a Priest at a Sacred Fig Tree (Chinnapura Village, 1967)

Figure 11. Iyengar Brahman Boy (L) and an Initiated Companion, with branches of bastard teak, on their way to the sacred fig tree (Bandipur, 1967)

Figure 12. Boy and His Companion at the Sacred Fig Tree: Branch of Bastard Teak set into the trunk of the tree (Bandipur, 1967)

Table 4. Plant Materials Used in Boys' Initiation Rituals

Botanical Name [English]	Kannada Name	Uses (*widespread practice)
Achyranthes aspera L.	uttaraNe-kaDDi	One of the 'nine sticks' required in the Smith caste ritual
Areca catechu Linn. [areca]	hombaaLe - 'flower'	Required for Farmer caste Daas boy's initiation at the riverside
Artocarpus heterophyllus Lam. [jackfruit]	haLasina-tooLe ('pieces of fruit', taken from inside the whole)	Required for initiation ritual at the riverside: Barber, Farmer, Washerman (*)

Table 4. Plant Materials Used in Boys' Initiation Rituals

Botanical Name [English]	Kannada Name	Uses (*widespread practice)
Azadirachta indica A. Juss. [neem]	*beevu* *beevin-kaDDi* 'small stick'	The Washerman & Barber caste custom is to "scratch the tongue" of the boy with this stick at the riverside initiation ritual. -The Barbers also touch the boy's right shoulder with the stick, while chanting "Govinda."
Bambusa arundinaceae [bamboo]	*bidiru/bambu bettada koolu-*	-'Cane sticks' required for Daas boys' initiation at the riverside: Barber, Farmer, Washerman (*)
Butea monosperma (Lam.) Taub [bastard teak, flame of the forest]	*muttugaDa-mara* 'tree' *danDin koolu* 'tip of branch'	-Held by Brahman boys as they make their initiation vows.(*) -Branch given to the boy by one who is already initiated. -Branch inserted into/onto a sacred fig tree. (*) -One of 'nine sticks' required in the Smith caste ritual
Calotropis gigantea (L.) R.Br. [Crown flower, Milkweed]	*(y)ekkada-kaDDi*	One of the 'nine sticks' required in the Smith caste ritual
Cassia fistula L. [Indian laburnum]	*kakke - huuvu* 'flower' *-soppugaLu* 'leaves'	Flowers: required for Farmer caste riverside initiation. Leaves: required for Barber and Washerman caste riverside initiations. (*)

Table 4. Plant Materials Used in Boys' Initiation Rituals

Botanical Name [English]	Kannada Name	Uses (*widespread practice)
Cicer arietinum Linn. [Bengal gram]	*kaDale*	Soaked, with jaggery, set on top of betel leaves, in Iyengar Brahman ritual Gram, distributed to participants in Iyengar Brahman ceremony at sacred fig tree. Powdered, given to boys in Smith caste ritual.
Curcuma longa L. [turmeric]	*arasiNa*	Whole rhizome required for *kankaNa* tied to the wrist of the boy *daasayya* in his marriage to the sacred fig tree. (*) Turmeric colored clothing, worn by Brahman and Smith caste boys. (*) Rhizomes pounded into powder by married women in the Iyengar ritual.
Cynodon dactylon Pers.	*garike*	Used in Iyengar Brahman ceremony for Ganesh.
Ficus glomerata Roxb. [country fig]	*atti-* (or) *hatti-kaDDi* 'stick'	One of the 'nine sticks' required in the Smith caste ritual
Ficus indica L. [banyan]	*aalada-* (or) *haalada-kaDDi* 'stick'	One of the 'nine sticks' required in the Smith caste ritual
Not identified	*toreenu-kaDDi*	One of the 'nine sticks' required in the Smith caste ritual

Table 4. Plant Materials Used in Boys' Initiation Rituals

Botanical Name [English]	Kannada Name	Uses (*widespread practice)
Not identified	*banni-kaDDi*	One of the 'nine sticks' required in the Smith caste ritual: a type of palm[45]
Mixture: Plantains, coconut, areca nuts		Offered as "alms" in Iyengar Brahman ceremony.
Others Areca nuts Betel leaves Coconut Jaggery Mango leaves Plantains Plantain leaf-plates		Used as in other ceremonies, as offerings to deities and to guests, for serving food (plantain leaves), to avert the 'evil eye' (smashing a coconut), and for purification (sprinkling with mango leaf)

Marriage Rituals

Marriage ceremonies consume large family resources. Most families are willing to make these expenditures, because family status is enhanced by a proper celebration. (Hanchett 1975) Careful attention goes into the selection of suitable partners for one's children, decisions about gift-giving, dowry (or bridewealth in some castes at the time of this research), other contributions from the bride's or bridegroom's families, setting the wedding date, uniting the bride and groom, feasting friends and relatives -- which can mean, for some local leaders, feasting the whole village -- and so on. The bride's and bridegroom's families have complex responsibilities on these

---

[45] Information from Malla Setty.

important occasions, of course; and the celebrations can go on for three or more days. Visits between the two groups of affines (in-laws) after marriage also involve mutually expected ritual exchanges of foods and other items.

At the time of this research rules for exchange between the bride's and bridegroom's families were in flux. "Dowry"– having the bride's family cover most costs, including expensive gifts to the bridegroom - - was not as universal as it now is. One Farmer caste man remarked to us in 1967 that "gift-giving is changing." He said that, "In former times the bridegroom's party was required to give many things (jewelry, clothing, large quantities of betel leaves and areca nuts, jaggery, rice, plantains), things to be used at the wedding. The bride would give the groom nothing. For the last two years," he continued, "the bride's family will pay for the wedding. If the bridegroom is educated, they must give him a watch and a gold chain. My son is SSLC-passed and working as a feed man. So the girls will come 'begging'." Apparently referring to the same trend, a Smartha Brahman told us that, "According to our rules, the boy's party should go in search of a girl, but nowadays the girl's party goes in search of a boy."

Wedding celebrations of Brahmans and non-Brahmans required help from other castes. Musicians and priests are needed by all; so there were three groups of professional musicians in the Bandipur Village Scheduled Caste Colony in 1966-1967. Priests would be Brahmans or *daasayyas, Aynorus* or other ritual specialists from the same caste as the bride's and bridegroom's families. Some families hire extra cooks to prepare and serve feasts. A bangle-seller is needed, and also some people to build the leafy canopy set in front of the bride's house, the place where the marriage is finalized.[46]. One Brahman man complained to us that, "Piper, cook, and fuel-breaker are considered to be more essential to a wedding than the priest. The priest position is no longer an honored one."

Figure 13. *Daasayya* Officiating at a Scheduled Caste Wedding, Bandipur

Figure 14. Scheduled Caste Musicians, Bandipur

As with other rites of passage, each caste and sub-caste has its own customs. However, there are many similarities among the rites of multiple groups; and certain plants and plant parts are common

---

[46] Like musical accompaniment, this job was a specialty of the Scheduled Caste in Bandipur Village at the time of this research study.

requirements. Our information on marriage rituals comes from in-depth interviews with members of 10 different castes or sub-castes[47] and direct observation of four weddings[48] in 1966- 1967. The following descriptions review some (but not all) of the basic rituals involved in planning and completing a marriage, with emphasis on the plant materials used.

Setting the wedding date: *lagnakaTTisu* ceremony. After the decision is made to go ahead with a marriage, an auspicious date needs to be selected. The date is selected by a ritual specialist assumed to have some knowledge of astrology. One Farmer man told us:

> If you want to arrange a marriage, first you go to a *purohit* [Brahman] with a **plantain, coconut, some betel-areca,** a *beNNuvaNNa,*[49] incense sticks, **turmeric**-vermillion, and camphor, and ask him to fix a date. He will consult the *Panchanga* to find a good date and time. He will write it on a piece of paper, put **turmeric** and vermillion on all four corners, and do *puja* worship for the paper. He will come to our house at the designated time to perform the marriage rituals.

Another Farmer caste (Mull subcaste) informant told us that the priest (referred to as *joyish*) will meet with representatives of the bride's and bridegroom's families, who present to him the above- mentioned items plus some **raw rice** and some coins (*dakshiNe*). He will fix an

---

[47] Washerman, Barber, Fisherman, Daas Okkaliga (Farmer), Mull Okkaliga (Farmer), Jogi Okkaliga (Farmer), Smartha Brahman, Iyengar Brahman, Smith (Achari), and Scheduled Caste (A.K.)

[48] Barber, Weaver, Shepherd, and Iyengar Brahman.

[49] A molded piece of cow dung with *garike* **grass** (*Cynodon dactylon*) in it, generally representing Ganesha, the remover of obstacles.

auspicious time and date and write it down in two copies (it is called *lagna patrike*). The people of the two families will exchange their papers with each other.

The date-setting event was more elaborately celebrated by Smith caste families and Brahmans. According to our Smith caste informant, the bridegroom's family goes to the bride's house on this occasion. In the party there must be nine people, he said, including three married women and one priest (*joyish*). They bring with them certain required items: five **coconuts**, five bunches (*chippu*) of **plantains**, five small tied bundles (*kaT*) of **betel leaves**, 1/4 kg. (1 *pow*) of **areca nuts,** one new sari, one new blouse piece for the bride, **flowers, turmeric** and vermillion. The girl is celebrated with a special *shaastra* by the married women, as she sits on a wooden platform (*hase maNe*), and plantains and areca nuts are distributed to all those present. As in the Farmer caste event, two copies of the agreement are then prepared, and the two families exchange their copies with each other. "Then," this person explained, "the boy's party returns to their village to get ready for the wedding."

Iyengar and Smartha Brahmans also do this ritual at the bride's house. The bridegroom's family, according to our Smartha Brahman informant, brings with them the following things, presenting them to the bride's family before meals: one bunch (*chippu*) of **plantains,** two **coconuts,** one blouse piece (*kaNa*), sandalwood sticks, incense and camphor. A meal is served, according to both castes' customs. Our information from Iyengar Brahmans describes the customary meal. Among the required items (cooked rice, etc.) **Bengal gram** is mentioned.[50] After the meal, the priest writes the *lagna patrike*

---

[50] The expected menu on this occasion among Iyengar Brahmans was said to include:

agreement in two copies, does *puja* worship for it, and gives it to the two parties, thus fixing the date. Both families conduct some preliminary rituals for the bride and bridegroom before the wedding.

Bringing waters to witness the marriage

An important part of all wedding ceremonies is the filling of some decorated, new clay pots with water. Called *airaNe*, these pots are filled at the river, carried back to the wedding house with much fanfare, and installed in a special room, where they receive worship and respect before, during and after a wedding. Among some groups, the wall above the filled pots is decorated with a drawing of a temple cart. (Figures 17 and 18) The procession to and from the river was accompanied by a vessel containing **areca flowers** carried by girls in the Shepherd and Scheduled Caste ceremonies that we observed.

A Farmer family of the Mull subcaste described the way that the groom's family collects and installs their pots, said to be filled with '*shaastra* water'. They make use of the areca flower; and their ritual includes pounding some **paddy**:

> Three married women put three *paDis* [1.5 *seer*] of **paddy** into a mortar. They invert the *paDi* two more times, explaining that "3+2=5," five being an auspicious number. As they pound the paddy, they sing special songs and put the pounded grain into a bamboo basket.

---

cooked rice with *saaru/sambar* made of pulses, three vegetable preparations (*tovve, palya, kosambari*), Bengal gram, green gram, crispy wafers (*happaLa/papadum*), *uppin kaayi* (spicy pickles), chutney, three snacks (*sanDige, obbaTTu, chitranna),* and sweet *paayasa.*

Figure 15. Filling *airaNe* Vessels at the River. Shephcrd caste wedding, Chinnapura 1967

Figure 16. Carrying *airaNe* Vessels back from the River: Scheduled Caste Wedding, Chinnapura 1967

63

The women then go in a procession with musicians to the river, carrying with them a small vessel and a mirror (*kaLasha-kannaDi*), in order to collect '*shaastra* water' from the river and summon Goddess Gangamma. At the river, they clean three new clay pots and fill them with water, setting them in front of a raised platform of sand. They tie a single thread (*honganulu*) around the three pots and put **turmeric** and vermillion on them.

On one plate they spread some **raw rice** and put the small vessel, now filled with water, on top of the rice. They insert **areca flowers** into the vessel, tie a thread around it, and put **turmeric** and vermillion on it. It is now called *kannikaLasha*.

Figure 17. *airaNe* Vessels in a Farmer Caste Wedding House, with a Bunch of Areca Flowers. (Chinnapura, 1967)

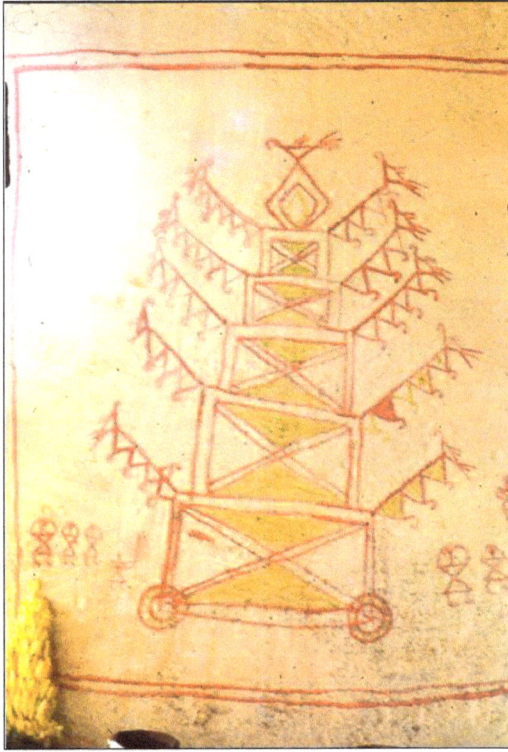

Figure 18. Drawing of a Temple Cart on Wall Above *airaNes*.
Farmer caster wedding, Chinnapura 1967

Three girls or women, walking side-by-side, carry the pots –
connected by the thread and by a twisted single dhoti -- on
their heads to the bridegroom's house. (Figure 16) In the
house, they set the pots on a platform (*gaddige*) under a picture
of a temple cart. In the platform, which was built of powdered
cow dung and water, a mixture of three grains were planted a
few days earlier; and the grains are starting to germinate:
paddy, finger millet, and **green gram**. The three pots, called
araNe, are set into three small holes in the platform. The
mouths of the pots are covered with small clay plates, and an
oil lamp is set on top of each one. "These lamps should be kept

65

burning until the bridegroom starts on his journey to the bride's house for the wedding." The three pots are honored with *puja* worship, which can be done by any female who is not a widow.

A Barber informant explained that only married women should carry the *airaNes* (they do five) back to the house – in this case, the wedding house, home of the bride. The women who carry the pots should be "the closest relatives" of the bride or bridegroom, we were told. After the wedding is over, a group of women will carry the pots to the village **sacred fig tree** and pour out the water at the base of the tree.

In a Shepherd wedding we observed that a specific flower, *Leucas indica* (Kannada *tumbe huuvu*), is required for the *puja* worship of the three pots of water. Each set of pots (three for the bride's family and three for the bridegroom's in this situation) had in front of it a plate with **areca flowers** on it. After the pots were installed in the household shrine, 12 kg. of rice **paddy** were put into a mortar pit on the floor. Pounding sticks (pestles) were decorated with vermillion, and a whole piece of **turmeric** was tied with a string (as a *kankaNa*) to each pounding stick. Three girls from the bridegroom's family pounded the paddy as four women sang a song. After the pounding was done, three girls used winnowing fans (*moRa*) to separate the rice grains from the chaff.

Preliminary ceremonies for the bride

In a Farmer caste home, the girl is seated on a wooden platform (*hase maNe*) for a 'lap-filling' (*maDilutumbu*) ceremony on the day before the wedding:

Her mother (or a maternal aunt, sister, or grandmother) first, and four other women – five married women in total, drop the following items from a tray into the front part (*seragu*) of the girl's sari: four or five bunches of **ripe plantains**, four or five **coconuts**, four or five wrapped packets (*kaT*) of **betel leaves**, along with four or five small cubes of jaggery (*chiTTachu*), four handfuls (*hiDis*) of **areca nut**, and four handfuls of **raw rice**.[51] The bride's hands are held palms up to receive the offerings.

Set on a plate in front of the bride is a plate spread with **raw rice**, on top of which is a small vessel (*kaLasha*). There is no water in the vessel, but the mouth is stuffed with as many **areca flowers** (*hombaaLe*) as can fit, "maybe even 100," I was told. Before the 'lap-filling', the tray of fruits etc. is set in front of this vessel and receives a gesture of respect *(namaskaara)*. After the 'lap-filling', each woman holds the vessel in her hands and circles it three times in front of the bride's face. Then she 'puts' handfuls of **raw rice** onto the girl's knees, shoulders, and the front part of the top of her head.[52]

The items from the girl's lap are bundled into a towel, which will be carried by a younger brother when the bride

---

[51] Discussing this ritual with a non-Brahman priest afterwards, I was told that it was a mistake to use quantities of four in this context. Five was the correct number, as it has auspicious connotations.

[52] I was told that this same ritual is done for a newly mature girl, but without the areca flower.

makes her first journey to her new husband's house. The package is called *kenchingaNTu.*

Among the Mull subcaste of Farmers, this ritual is called *viLLe shaastra,* or 'betel leaf *shaastra'.* It is done at the girl's house a few days after the marriage date is set. The groom's party goes to the girl's house, carrying three **coconuts,** three bunches *(chippu)* of **ripe plantains,** five cubes of **jaggery,** three packets *(kaT)* of **betel leaves,** three fistfuls of **areca nuts,** and **flowers.** They also bring a sari and a blouse. The girl is seated on a wooden platform while married women of her family do the *shaastra* for her. Betel nuts are distributed to those present, and a meal is served to the boy's party. After the meal, the two families discuss the "give and take" to be transacted for the wedding.

The Barber caste custom is to do this ceremony in the evening before the wedding, after the bridegroom's party has arrived in the girl's village. They also it 'betel leaf *shaastra'* (*iLLe/viLLe shaastra*). Their required items for the 'lap-filling', done by married women, are: **betel leaves, areca nuts, plantains, raw rice.** Items set into the bride's lap also include: one *paDi* (1.5 *kg.*) of **Bengal gram,** one **dry coconut** *(kobbari),* and three pieces of **jaggery.**[53] After the ritual, the family distributes betel-areca and puffed **Bengal gram** to all those present.

In Chinnapura Village, we observed a Shepherd caste family's 'lap-filling' ceremony for the bride done two days before the wedding.

---

[53] These notes may not be complete. They do not indicate what is done with the plantains, rice, and areca nuts.

Figure 19. Pounding Paddy
Before a Marriage (Scheduled
Caste, Chinnapura, 1967)

Figure 20. Iyengar Bride Seated in front
of a Grinding Stone before Her Marriage
(Bandipur, 1966)

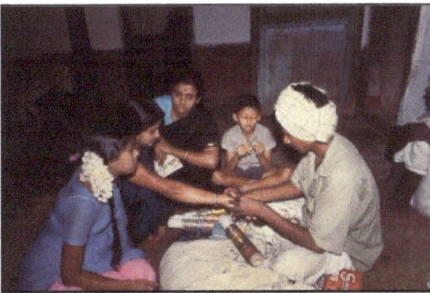

Figure 21. An Iyengar Bride Putting on
New Glass Bangles (Bandipur, 1966)

Figure 22. Three Small Cubes
of Jaggery, called *chiTTAchu*
(courtesy of Nikita Chandan)

This group called the ritual 'mother's house sitting' (*taayi mane hase*):

> The girl sat on a folded wool blanket, indoors, near the front door of her house. With her on the blanket were five small piles of **raw rice**. In front of her was a plate of

69

betel-areca and a plate with **plantains, coconuts, raw rice** and other things, alongside a small vessel (*kaLasha*) with betel leaves, and *hombaale.*[54] Her mother and some young girls did *namaskaara* to the plates, putting vermillion on them and also on the girl's forehead.

The plate with coconuts and plantains was put on her lap, and the vessel circled around in front of her. And **raw rice** was 'put' on her feet, knees, elbows, shoulders and head. The young girls then waved a plate of red liquid in front of her as *aarati*, to avoid the 'evil eye'.

Both Smartha and Iyengar Brahmans celebrate the girl by tying a 'birth house *taaLi*' pendant (*huTTidamane taaLi* or *kanya taaLi*) on her before the groom arrives in her village. The girl, wearing a sari presented by her mother's brother, is seated on a wooden platform. Some married women put **turmeric-colored rice** (*akśate*) on her forehead and **areca nuts** into her hands. A married woman (her mother, in the Iyengar ritual we observed) ties the *taaLi* on her. Putting on new glass bangles is another celebration for the bride.

Preliminary ceremonies for the bridegroom

Those castes for which we have information all perform special rites for the bridegroom at some time before the marriage. Among castes that wear the sacred thread, the groom puts on a fresh, new thread before the wedding.

---

[54] Our notes do not specify which type of hombaaLe flower this is, but it is very likely to be areca flower, which seems to be preferred for auspicious occasions, such as marriage.

Among Brahmans the preliminary ritual honoring the bridegroom is called *vaara puja* (Smartha) or *maduvaNiga shaastra* (Iyengar). The Iyengars seat the bridegroom on a wooden platform, and married women smear oil and turmeric powder on him. He is then bathed, and a meal is served to friends and relatives. A priest officiates at the Smartha ceremony, conducted in the evening before the wedding, and special snacks (*tambiTTu*) are distributed to guests.

The custom among the Smith caste is to do the bridegroom's ceremony two days before the wedding, after the special canopy (*pandal*) has been erected in front of his house. The boy takes a bath and sets his clothes in front of the household God while offering worship at the household shrine. After food is served to friends and relatives, the bridegroom puts on his new clothes and sits on the special wooden platform. The married women who are present put vermillion and *vibhuti* (sacred ash) on his forehead, one-by-one. This ritual is called *haNegiDuva shaastra*. Among the Barbers, the bridegroom (called *maduvaNiga*) is seated on a wooden platform in front of a small vessel containing water (*kaLasha*), with leaves and a coconut set in its mouth. Like others, he also is honored by married women, who take **raw rice** in both hands and 'put' it on him, touching their fists on his knees, shoulders, and head, and leaving most of the rice on his head. After this they "salute" him (offer *namaskaara*) and put a flower garland on him.

We observed a bridegroom's ritual during the evening before a Shepherd caste marriage in Chinnapura Village. (A similar rite had already been performed for the bride the day before):

> The bridegroom was seated on a wooden platform (*hase maNe*)
> in the marriage house, home of the bride. Some young

71

girls were responsible for honoring him on this occasion. He was given a "bag" – actually a large cloth, tied up by the bride, who had emptied a plate into it – containing **coconut, plantains, betel-areca, and raw rice.** A girl picked up a large handful of **rice** from the cloth, put it back into the plate, and then spilled it out again; this was done two or three times. The girl performing this ritual then handed a betel-areca set and two plantains to the groom, who lifted the items up quickly to his right shoulder and handed them back to her. This was done three times.

A mixture of **turmeric** and oil was smeared thoroughly over the bridegroom's cheeks, palms, shins, and the tops of his feet.

The bridegroom then got a shave from a Barber, and one of the daughters of the house gave him a bath. (One member of the group present commented that he should have bathed <u>before</u> the turmeric-oil smearing, not after it.)[55]

The Fisherman caste ritual for the bridegroom is similar to those just described, but not identical. They call it *hase śaastra* or *modal hase*, and it is done at the boy's house three days before the wedding. (The girl's party does not participate.)

---

[55] A bath after the shaving is, however, customary, because the Barber's touch is considered by most castes to be polluting. (Helen Ullrich and Shalini Bhat, personal communication)

The bridegroom is seated on a special wooden platform, and three married women do the shaastra for him as family members, friends, and neighbors look on. They set a small vessel (*kannikaLasha*) in front of him. In the mouth of this vessel are set some **betel leaves** and **areca flowers** (*hombaale*). Next to it are a mirror, and a collection of things (*cence gaNTu koDuvudu*) bundled up in a white cloth: two bunches (*chippu*) of **plantains**, two **coconuts**, two *pow* (½ kg.) of **areca nuts**, one bundle (*kaT*) of **betel leaves**, and some coins (4 *annas* = one *paavli*).

The women sing special "Sobbane Songs"[56] and wave the vessel in a clockwise direction in front of him. He is asked to touch the bundle of fruits and to give respect to it. The married women 'put' rice on him, and he puts some coins and areca nuts into a plate as a gesture of thanks. After this the boy's friends and relatives give him presents.

Farmers of the Mull group do the bridegroom's ritual one day before the wedding at the boy'shouse: collecting their pots of water from the river and installing them in the house, the family will have food. [That same day, or the next,] a Barber will be summoned to give the boy a shave. He then bathes and puts on new clothes. "The rice that was used in writing the hase" is thrown on his

---

[56] Songs for a newly matured girl also are Sobbana Songs, as mentioned above.

head.[57] Married women then do aarathi for the bridegroom. A strictly vegetarian meal is served before the bride-groom's party starts their journey to the bride's village for the wedding.

Grinding and pounding food grains

As previously discussed, the Shepherd and Mull Okkaliga Farmer caste vessel-filling rituals are preceded by some ceremonial pounding of rice.

Just as people undergo ritual transitions when they move from one stage of life to another, so also grains require complex processing to become foods. Some of the rituals just described include pounding of food grains with the household mortar and pestle commonly found in village kitchens at the time of this research. In an Iyengar Brahman wedding we observed, grinding granulated wheat (*rave*) and turmeric was central to rituals for both bridegroom and bride. (Figure 20)[58] One ritual we observed proceeded as follows:

A decorated grinding stone and two pounding sticks were placed in front of the groom. He was seated between his brother and his brother's wife. Two cow dung images of Ganesh (Vigneshwara) with grass in them had been placed in front of the grinding stone. Music began. Five married women from the groom's side stood, offered

---

[57] Writing the *hase'* refers to sme rice that had been spread on the bridegroom's sitting place: a short hymn or holy saying, such as '*om'* or *Shri GaNeshaya naama*, has been written on it with the right hand middle finger. (Narayan Hegde, personal communication)

[58] Our notes relate to the ceremony for the groom in this marriage, but our photo (Figure 20) shows the bride's house grinding stone ritual.

worship to the God, and then poured some granulated **wheat** (*rave*) and **turmeric** into the grinding stone. The women pounded the turmeric with the two sticks and ground up the mixture with the grinding stone. The women then did *aarathi* for the groom, his brother's wife, and finally for his brother, each of whom put a coin into the *aarathi* plate.

The bridegroom's arrival

Marriages among all castes took place in the bride's home village at the time of this study. The bridegroom arrived in the village with his parents and other relatives and friends, staying at least two days in a room or house, called *biDade mane*, that had been arranged for them. The bride's party welcomed them with great fanfare, fed them, and did everything they could to make their stay comfortable. We participated in one Iyengar Brahman welcoming event in Bandipur (1966), and we collected information on the welcoming customs of seven other castes. Our best description of the welcoming event comes from a woman of the Mull Okkaliga Farmer subcaste:

> The boy's party arrives, usually in the evening before the wedding, carrying three baskets of presentations for the bride and a small vessel (*kaLasha*). They bring to the bride the following things: jewels, clothes, **raw rice, coconuts, betel leaves, areca nuts,** and prepared snacks called *tambiTTu* or *tamTa*.

> The boy's party will not enter the girl's village directly. They first sit in a place that has been prepared for them: in a

75

temple, in a village school, or under a **sacred fig tree**, on mats or carpets set out by the bride's party.[59]

The girl's party comes, with musical accom-paniment, to ask about their travel experience and safe arrival. There must be some married women in the welcoming group, which carries along a small vessel and a mirror (*kaLasha-kannaDi*). They may also bring ripe plantains, clarified butter, and coffee or milk. The girl's party gives the boy's party some water to wash their hands, face, and feet. And they give juice and water to drink. They present all married women in the boy's party with **turmeric** and vermillion and flowers.

Everyone now goes to the bride's house, where the groom is honored under the canopy of front. The groom's party is carrying their baskets of gifts; and these baskets receive *aarathi* along with the groom (and his horse, if he is riding a horse). The purpose of *aarathi* is to remove the 'evil eye'.

Water with **turmeric** in it is thrown on the ground, and a spot of the mud thus formed goes onto the bridegroom's forehead. Some married women put water on the feet of the boy, and the bridegroom's whole party is invited inside the wedding house.

Once inside the house, the bridegroom goes immediately to the place where the *araNe* water pots are kept and makes

---

[59] This informant said that the boy may be riding a horse.

a 'salute' to them. The baskets of gifts are set in front of the water pots. The girl is called to stand there, and the bridegroom's party presents their gifts to her.

Other castes' welcoming rituals are generally similar. The Iyengar bridegroom's party arrival celebration that we joined in Bandipur involved going with musicians to the roadside bus stand, as the bridegroom's party had arrived from Coorg on a bus. There was a plan to visit the **sacred fig tree** at the entrance to the village, but it started to rain. So they were escorted to a two-room structure, called Vedanta Sabha, instead. On the path, the bride's mother put a welcoming garland on the groom and some **turmeric** and vermillion on his forehead. She handed him **two coconuts with turmeric** on them and some betel-areca. **Turmeric** and vermillion were offered to the married women in the bridegroom's party, and scent was sprinkled on the whole group from a small silver container. At the Vedanta Sabha, coffee and some snacks (*rave upiTTu and maisuur paak*) were served to all, as the visitors rested up from their journey.

A verbal description of an Iyengar welcoming ceremony mentions that the bridegroom's party must bring along with them the following items for the bride: five **coconuts**, five bunches of **plantains**, five **dry coconuts** (*kobbari*), five packets (*kaT*) of **betel leaves**, **areca nuts**, clothes, and jewels. One special plate has on it a square of **jaggery** (*bellada accu*) with some **cumin** sprinkled on it. On top of this they will place the marital pendant, the *taaLi*. Also included among their presentations are some food items[60] and a **whole turmeric rhizome** (*arasiNadakone*).

---

[60] Fried **Bengal gram**, avalakki (pounded rice), hasikaDli-kaaLu, goDambi, draakshi (raisins), sweets, and candy.

77

After initially welcoming the bridegroom's party with musical accompaniment, this report continues, the bride's parents will escort them to the place where they will stay. It is "compulsory," we were told, to serve the steamed preparation called *idLi* to the bridegroom's party after they are settled.

Creating the marriage bond (*muhurta, muhurtam,* or *dhaare*)

The formal union of bride and groom usually takes place the next morning, after some preliminary rituals. Among the "twice- born" castes, whose men wear a sacred thread, the groom will have put on a new thread. Several castes do a small drama, called *Kashi Yatre*, in which the bridegroom sets off for Benares (Kashi), as a *brahmacharya*, only to be summoned by the bride's parents, who ask him come back and marry their daughter. In the Weaver caste wedding we observed, the young man set off "for Kashi" with two little girls, one of whom was carrying a small vessel (*kaLasha*) filled with **areca flowers**. After he agreed to return to the wedding, the bride's mother poured water as the bride's father gratefully washed his feet. Just before his marriage rites began, he sat on a wooden platform and changed his sacred thread. An Iyengar Brahman wedding we observed included an elaborate initiation-style ceremony for the bridegroom at the riverside in front of a carefully tended sacred *homa* fire; he too set off for Kashi and had to be summoned back for the wedding.

A Barber caste bride and groom are united in the presence of a small vessel (*kaLasha*), which is set in front of nine small leaf containers, each filled with a specific seed or grain (*daana*). The **nine grains or seeds** are raw rice, horse gram (*huraLi*), cumin, green gram, tur Dal (*togari*), Bengal gram, sesame, black gram, and granulated wheat (*rave*). Some ripe plantains, betel-areca and a special **flower, crepe jasmine** (*nanjabatlahuuvu*),[61] also are part of the setting.

A **turmeric rhizome** tied with threads (*kankaNa*) to their wrists is customary among Barbers and other castes. A **betel leaf** also may be tied as a *kankaNa*.

The formal union of the bride and groom among all castes is marked by three specific ritual actions: (1) **exchange of flower garlands,** (2) tying of a *taaLi* necklace on the bride, and (3) pouring a liquid over the joined hands of the bride and bridegroom, to bless the union.[62]

A verbal description of a Smartha Brahman *muhurtam* lists the specific steps that unite the bride and groom. This sequence is generally similar to other castes' customs, though no two castes do any of this in exactly the same way:

> The groom stands on a wooden platform, and the bride's mother's brother brings her to stand on another wooden platform in front of him.
>
> A curtain (called *antarapaTa*) is held up between the bride and groom.
>
> The priest (*joyish*) chants mantras as the curtain is slowly removed, and he hands a garland to each of them,

---

[61] According to Helen Ullrich (personal communication), *nanjabatlahuuvu* is crepe jasmine (*Ervatamia divaricata*).

[62] According to Helen Ullrich and Shalini Bhat, pouring water on a gift signifies that the bond created is irrevocable – a reference in this case to the permanence of the marriage bond. (personal communication)

instructing them to exchange their garlands, doing the 'putting of family relationship garlands' (*sambhand-hamaale haak-uvudu*).

The bride and groom put **cumin** and **jaggery** on each other's heads. (This is not a common practice in other castes' weddings.)

The priest asks the bride and groom to put their hands together, and '*dhaare* water' (*dhaare niiru*) is poured over their hands.[63]

There is some ritual conversation between the fathers of the bride and groom after they both repeat mantras chanted by the priest. The bride's father says: 'I brought up my daughter to this age. From this time onwards, for the continuity and prosperous growth of your heritage, to my heart's content and with the witness of *Agni* [fire], I hand her to you'. The groom's father replies: 'According to your words, we will not give her any trouble for her whole life. We will look after her in a good way. For the continuity of my family line, I will take this girl to my son. I accept this for my son with the witness of *Agni* [fire] and *asTdikpaalakas*.[64]

---

[63] Among the Havik Brahmans of Shimoga District, the dhare pouring custom is for the couple first to hold hands with the bride's hands touching the coconut. Before the liquid is poured, however, they shift the hold, so that the groom's hands are touching it. (Helen Ullrich, personal communication)

[64] Gods of all the directions: north, south, east, west, northeast, southeast, northwest, and southwest (Malla Setty information).

The bride and groom now sit on the same wooden platform, as a plate with the *taaLi* is taken around the room to be blessed by all those present.

The priest then asks permission of the people to tie the *taaLi*, and the bridegroom ties it on the neck of the bride.[65]

It is customary in some castes for the priest to tie a special thread around the bride and groom during this ceremony.

Figure 23. A Bridegroom, Bringing a Sari, Areca Flowers, and Other Items, is Welcomed at the Bride's House (Weaver caste, 1967)

Figure 24. Pouring Milk and Clarified Butter over the Newly Married Couples' Hands (Weaver caste, Bandipur, 1967)

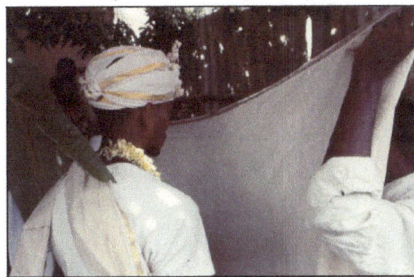

Figure 25. Curtain Separating the Bride and Groom, just before they exchange garlands (Weaver caste, Bandipur, 1967)

---

[65] The order of actions may be slightly different among other groups. Some tie the *taaLi* before liquid is poured over the couple's joined hands.

81

Among most non-Brahmans and the Scheduled Caste, the couple hold a single coconut in their joined hands for *dhaare*. The liquid is a mixture of milk and clarified butter (in Kannada, *haal- tuppa*). (Figure 24) It is poured by other married couples. Our notes suggest that the Brahmans do the pouring differently, using some kind of special water, called *dhaare niiru*; and they may not have the bride and groom hold a coconut.

Figure 26. *Phala Puja* with Tender Coconuts and Areca Flowers. Farmer Caste Wedding, Chinnapura 1967

A ritual performed among Brahmans and some other castes after the *dhaare* is called by the Sanskrit name, *phaala puja* or 'worship of fruits'. (We have a verbal report of the Barber caste doing this ritual, and we observed it in a Farmer caste wedding (Figure 26). It consists of setting five **tender coconuts** and ripe plantains in front of the bride and groom. The priest asks the bride to offer worship to the coconuts and sprinkle water on them with a **mango leaf**, as he chants mantras, according to an Iyengar verbal report. For the Barbers, the required items are five tender coconuts, some **raw rice** and a **plantain leaf**. Their report states that the priest (who would be a local Brahman) does worship for this.

There are several other rituals customarily performed after the *dhaare/muhurtam*. Some of them involve a **sacred fig tree**. Among the Scheduled Caste, for example, it is customary for the bride and groom to go directly to a sacred fig tree after the *taaLi* has been tied. According to a leader of this community, a group of married women blesses the new couple as they sit under the tree; and then the bride and groom bless each other.

Among the Barbers, the custom is for the newly married bride and groom to go to a **sacred fig tree** later on, after they have had a meal. Seated on a wooden platform, they put their hands outo a pile of **raw rice;** and the **turmeric rhizome** *kankaNas* are removed from their wrists. These *kankaNas* are then tied to a branch of the tree. This ceremony, which we observed at the riverside in Chinnapura, also requires a special flower: the *tumbe huuvu* (**Leucas indica**). In fact, the ritual is called the *tumbe huuvindhaare šaastra*, suggesting perhaps that it is the flower and the tree which are getting married. After the *kankaNas* have been put onto the tree, relatives of the couple pour the customary mixture of milk and clarified butter at the base of the tree trunk. After some mutual back- and-forth between the bride and groom, the bride putting vermillion onto the groom's hands three times, the couple tuck **betel-areca** sets into each other's clothes and hair, and then tuck one packet of it into the bark of the tree's trunk.

Like the Barbers, the Shepherd family whose wedding we observed also untied their **turmeric**-and-thread *kankaNas* under the **sacred fig tree**, attaching them to the tree, and poured some milk with clarified butter (*haal-tuppa*) at the base of the tree.

The Farmers of the Mull subcaste told us that they also do a ritual at the riverside **sacred fig tree** after their post-wedding meal. The bride and groom sit together under the tree, and the bride washes the feet of the groom with purifying cow dung and water, somehow using a *Leucas indica* flower (*tumbe huuvu*) for this *puja*. Next she prostrates to her husband, and the groom then washes the hands of the bride.

It is customary for a Barber caste family to have married women to go in a procession, with musicians, carrying the *airaNe* water pots to a **sacred fig tree**. After circumambulating the tree three times, they pour the water out of the pots onto the base of the tree trunk.

A member of the Smith caste told us that it is customary for their group for the bride and groom to play a little game after they have completed their unification rituals. It is called *todkinakki*. The groom puts his gold ring into a new clay pot containing **five kinds of grain** and some areca nut. Married women watch gleefully as the bride and groom compete three times to find the ring in the pot of grains. The five kinds of grain they mentioned were: raw rice, tur Daal, Bengal gram, green gram, and black gram. After this food is served to all the friends and relatives who are present, and "the *muhurta* is now over."

The wedding canopy

In preparation for the marriage, leafy canopies (*chapra*) are constructed in front of both the bride's and the groom's homes. The bride's house canopy is built to welcome the bridegroom's party when they arrive. The canopy in front of the groom's house is built in preparation for the arrival of the bride's party later on.[66]

We do not have many details about this structure, except to note that in the Barber caste wedding we observed, "The most important part of the *chapra*" was said to be a stake of **country fig** (*Ficus glomerata*) "planted in the earth." This pole received special decoration and worship from the bride and bridegroom after wedding rituals were all completed.

Ritual exchanges after a marriage

Marriage of their children creates important bonds between two extended families. These bonds result in various kinds of mutual help, possibly some quarreling, and always involve ritual exchanges. The travels of a bride between her natal home and her husband's home, especially in the early years of a marriage, entail carrying certain gifts back and forth. For example, An Iyengar Brahman woman told me that when she visits her daughter's marital home for the first time, she will be presented with a new winnowing fan (*moRa*) containing **five kinds of food grains**, a comb, a silk blouse piece, some vermillion, a mirror and bangles. The five kinds of food grains include: **tur Daal, Bengal gram, raw rice, green gram,** and **wheat**[67]. The visiting mother

---

[66] Helen Ullrich, personal communication.

[67] The absence of finger millet (*raagi*) is interesting, considering its importance in the daily diet of the non-Brahmans of this place.

must bring snack preparations, numbering five of each type, this woman told me.

Summary: Plants in Marriage Rituals

In this general overview of multiple castes' marriage customs a few plants figure prominently. Of particular importance is the **areca flower** (*hombaaLe*), which appears at all steps of the process. We did not always make written notes documenting it while observing the ceremonies, but our pictures leave no doubt of its importance in almost all marriage rituals.

The **sacred fig tree** also is an integral part of marriage rituals: as a welcoming place for a bridegroom, and as a witness to the union of the newly married couple. There are hints of "tree marriage" in some castes' rituals concluding the marriage: pouring the milk-clarified butter mixture at its base and tying the bride's and groom's turmeric bracelets (*kankaNa*) onto the tree's branch.

In rituals at the sacred fig tree and elsewhere (collecting water for the ancestral vessels, *airaNe*) the flower called *tumbe huuvu* (*Leucas indica*) also is required in several castes' rituals.

Familiar from all other rituals, **raw rice** and **coconuts** also are necessities for weddings. The universal non-Brahman custom is to pour milk and clarified butter over a ripe coconut held by the bride and groom's joined hands. And tender, green coconuts are used in the ceremony called *phala puja* in some castes' rituals soon after the couple has been formally united in marriage.

Pounding and grinding of **grains** and turmeric are part of several castes' customary marriage rituals. And **mixtures of grains** are mentioned in a few verbal reports, such as the Mull Okkaliga (Farmer) custom of having some grains germinate in the platform where the ancestral vessels are to be set, or the required presentations to a new bride's mother among Iyengar Brahmans on the occasion of the first visit to her daughter's marital home.

Familiar plant items from other rites of passage include **Bengal gram, whole turmeric rhizome, turmeric powder,** and **jaggery.** And specific quantities of **betel leaves** and **areca nuts** are required in some marriage rituals of all castes. **Mango leaves** are used to sprinkle purifying water in some groups' rituals. Table 5 lists the principal plants and plant parts of importance in these marriage rituals. **Flowers** are used in many ways, especially in the flower garland-exchange that unifies a bride and bridegroom.[68]

---

[68] There surely are required flowers for these garlands, but our notes do not have information on this topic. Flowers chosen depend on the season and what flowers are available. (Helen Ullrich, personal communication)

Table 5. Symbolic Uses of Plant Materials in Marriage Rituals

Botanical Name	Kannada Terms & Translations	Uses (* widespread)
	Mixture of 'grains': rice paddy, finger millet, and green gram	Grains germinated in the platform on which *airaNe* vessels sit (Mull Okkaliga) during the whole the marriage
	Mixture: raw rice, *togari beeLe,* Bengal gram, green gram, black gram (*Phaseolus mungo*)	Mixture used in playful bride-groom competition, searching for a gold ring in a small pot (Smith caste)
	Mixture of 'grains': *togari beeLe* (*Cajanus cajang*), Bengal gram, raw rice, green gram (*Phaseolus aureus*), and wheat	Presented to a newly married woman's mother when she first visits her daughter's marital home (Iyengar Brahman)
Areca catcheu [areca]	*aDike* 'areca nut'	-Bridegroom's party brings areca nuts to the date-setting ceremony(*) -Areca nuts are a required item for 'lap-filling' shaastra for the bride.(*)
	hombaaLe (or) *huuvu* 'flower'	-Clusters of areca flowers, set into the mouth of a *kaLasha* vessel, are part of every wedding ritual (*)
Cajanus cajang [tur Daal]	*togari beeLe*	-One of 'five grains' in small game after the wedding (Smith caste) -One of 'five grains' presented to a child's new mother-in-law (Iyengar Brahman)

Table 5. Symbolic Uses of Plant Materials in Marriage Rituals

Botanical Name	Kannada Terms & Translations	Uses (* widespread)
Cicer arietinum [Bengal gram]	*kaDale - beeLe* 'gram' (split) -*kaaLu* (whole) -*puri* (puffed)	-One of the required items for bride's 'lap- filling' ceremony (*) -Puffed gram distributed to guests after lap- filling ceremony for bride before a wedding (Barber) -One of 'nine grains' that witness a Barber caste wedding -One of five food grains presented to a child's mother-in-law (Iyengar)
Cocos nucifera [coconut]	*tenginkaayi* 'ripe coconut' *iLLeniiru* 'tender coconut' *kobbari* 'dry coconut' (meat removed from the shell and dried)	-Bridegroom's party brings ripe coconuts to the date-setting (*) -Coconuts are a required item for 'lap-filling' shaastra for the bride.(*) -Ripe coconut(s) held by bride and groom together, as they receive blessings from well- wishers, who pour a mixture of milk and clarified butter over the coconut and their hands.(*) -Tender coconuts, used in *Phala Puja* (*)
Cuminum cyminum [cumin]	*jiirige*	-Mixed with raw rice and sesame seeds, used in Barber caste marriage: bride and groom put the mixture on each other's heads. -Carried with jaggery when the Iyengar Brahman groom travels to the bride's village home. Marital *taaLi* set on some cumin after the groom's arrival. -Smartha Brahman bride and groom put mixture of cumin and jaggery on each other's heads after the *muhurtham*.

Table 5. Symbolic Uses of Plant Materials in Marriage Rituals

Botanical Name	Kannada Terms & Translations	Uses (* widespread)
Curcuma longa [turmeric]	*arasiNa -pudi* 'powdered turmeric' *-kone* 'whole rhizome'	-Whole turmeric rhizome is tied with a string to the ritual pounding sticks in the Shepherd caste ceremony for ancestral water pots (*araNe).* -A mixture of turmeric and oil is smeared on the bride and the groom at their respective ceremonies before their marriage.(*) -A whole turmeric rhizome is tied to the wrists of the bride and groom with a special thread (*kankaNa*). This may be later hung on a branch of the sacred fig tree.
Cynodon dactylon [a grass]	*garike*	Used in marriage arrangement, inserted into a cow dung shape, representing Ganesh.
Ervatamia divaricata [crepe jasmine]	*nanjabatlahu uvu*	Used to decorate setting with *kaLasha* vessel at Barber wedding.
Ficus glomerata [country fig]	*atti (or) hatti mara*	Post used in wedding canopy
Ficus religiosa [sacred fig tree]	*araLimara*	-Visited after the marriage is finalized. -May hold the marital *kankaNa* bracelets. -Water from *airaNe* vessels is poured at the base of the tree after the wedding (Barber)

Table 5. Symbolic Uses of Plant Materials in Marriage Rituals

Botanical Name	Kannada Terms & Translations	Uses (* widespread)
Leucas indica	*tumbehuuvu* 'flower'	-Used in Shepherd caste ceremony for filling *airaNe* vessels -*KeravaaLa šaastra* (Okkaliga) at riverside after the *dhaare* -Used in ceremony under a sacred fig tree (Barbers)
Musa sapientum [plantain]	*baaLe haNNu* 'ripe plantains'	-Bridegroom's party brings ripe plantains to the date-setting ceremony(*) -Ripe plantains are a required item for 'lap- filling' shaastra for the bride.(*)
Oryza sativa [rice]	*bhatta* 'rice paddy' *akki* 'raw rice'	-Raw rice is a required item for the 'lap-filling' shaastra for a bride.(*)
	akšate 'turmeric-colored raw rice'	-Pounding rice paddy is a preliminary to the Mull Okkaliga (Farmer caste) ritual of collecting water for ancestral vessels -The *kaLasha* vessel in some rituals sits on top of a bed of raw rice -A bed of raw rice is part of the sacred fig tree ritual after the wedding. -Turmeric-colored raw rice is thrown on people (brides, grooms, guests, relatives) as a gesture of blessing (*) -Hands full of raw rice are used to bless the bride and groom in the 'rice putting' action.
Piper betle [betel]	*viLyadele* 'betel leaf'	-Bridegroom's party brings betel leaves to the date-setting ceremony(*) -Betel leaves are a required item for 'lap- filling' shaastra for the bride.(*) -A betel leaf may be tied to a bride or bridegroom's wrist as a *kankaNa*.

91

Table 5. Symbolic Uses of Plant Materials in Marriage Rituals

Botanical Name	Kannada Terms & Translations	Uses (* widespread)
Saccharum.... [sugar]	*bella* 'jaggery' *chiTTachu* 'small cube of jaggery	Brought with the bridegroom, when he arrives in the bride's village. Used in preliminary ceremonies for both bride and groom.
	-sesame -black gram/*uddu* (*Phaseolus mungo* Linn.) -granulated wheat/*rave*	
Triticum aestivum [wheat]	*rave* 'granulated wheat'	Ground with grinding stones in Iyengar ceremonies for both bride and groom at their homes before a wedding.
Mixture of Nine Grains/Seeds (*navadaanya*)	-raw rice/*akki* -horse gram/*huraLi* (*Macrotyloma uniflorum* Lam.) -cumin/*jiirige* -green gram/*hesaru beeLe* (*Phaseolus aureus* Roxb.) -tur Dal/*togari* (*Cajanus cajang* (L.) Millspaugh -Bengal gram/*kaDale*	Each grain/seed is in a leaf-cup container, the row of nine containers set behind a *kaLasha* vessel during Barber caste wedding ceremony.

Pregnancy Rituals

A woman usually returns to her natal home for confinement after completing six or seven months of pregnancy, especially for her first one or two pregnancies. Her husband's family provides her with new clothes on this occasion, and she carries some food gifts (*y)ecca*) with her. If her parents cannot afford to maintain her during her stay, the husband's family will help out. She returns to her husband's house when her new baby is three to five months old, so the stay in her natal home lasts from five to seven months.

We have information on the customary practices of six castes: Smith, Fisherman, Farmer, Iyengar Brahman, and Smartha Brahman, and Scheduled Caste (A.K.). All but the Fisherman perform a ceremony for the expectant mother before her departure. Someone will have come to escort her to her natal home – perhaps her parents, or a sibling. These ceremonies combine features of maturation and marriage rituals already described, with certain additions.

A pregnant woman of the Smith caste, for example, is seated on a small wooden platform (*hase maNe*) as some married women rub her cheeks with a mixture of **turmeric** and oil (*arasineNNe*). After this, she takes an oil bath and puts on a new sari and blouse. Then she and the married women do *puja* for a bundle of bangles, and the bangle-seller puts new bangles on her and on her married women companions.[69] Next, she sits next to her husband on wooden platforms while others sprinkle them with **turmeric-colored rice** (*akšate*). After a special meal is served to the family and in-laws, she goes to her natal home. The married women who help her during this ritual are offered a collection

---

[69] According to my 1976 assistant, H. Malathi, many Karnataka castes (but not all) customarily put on green bangles during the seventh month pregnancy ritual.

of items: turmeric, vermilion, flowers, and **areca nuts.** If any boys are in the group, they get some **Bengal gram-flour.**

A Farmer family told us that the pregnant woman's mother-in-law will do the 'lap-filling' ceremony (*maDilutumbu*) for her, as she sits on a blanket on a wooden plank. The special items offered to her are one tied packet (*kaT*) of **betel leaves,** some flowers, **rice paddy, plantains,** and **coconut.** When she goes to her natal home for confinement, she brings along some foods needed to cook a meal, but no salt.[70]

The Smartha Brahman custom, as described to us, is to celebrate the expectant mother's first two pregnancies by inviting five married women and conducting "a bangle ceremony." The pregnant woman receives an offering reminiscent of that of the Farmer family just described, with additional requirements that there be **five kinds of fruits** and a **coconut with the fibrous outer covering and outer coat** (mesocarp and endocarp) still on it. She also gets some areca nut and betel leaves, a sari, and a blouse piece.

Among Iyengar Brahmans some boys are asked to go to village trees and collect **three kinds of leaf buds: banyan, sacred fig, and country fig.** These buds are rubbed together into a paste in a bowl (*kalpattu*) used to mix Ayurvedic medicines by some virgin girls, as a priest chants mantras. The expectant mother and her husband are seated on *hase* wooden platforms after she has had an oil bath. Her mother-in-law hold her head, face tilted upward, as her husband

---

[70] In Chinnapura Village, one Farmer house "sent-off" their daughter-in-law to her natal home, even though it was only a few houses away in the same village. Nonetheless, her husband's three sisters came from another town, where they lived, to "send her off" with proper rituals. She brought with her some *dose* – a large rice and gram pancake – prepared in her husband's family kitchen.

squeezes some of the liquid from the paste through a cloth into her nostrils. The explanation we were given was that this filtered mixture enters directly into the baby's mouth; and when he/she gets it, the baby knows that "it will be born into a Brahman house."

Among the Scheduled Caste families, the ceremony for the pregnant woman is called *hosage šaastra*. She wears a new sari, and she is seated on a *hase maNe* platform as two rituals are performed for her: 'lap filling' and 'putting rice' (touching her shoulders etc. with **raw rice**). A special meal is served to her and the relatives who have come to take her to her natal home. The group that leaves with her brings some snacks with them: *vaDe, cakkali, and dose.*

In three castes for whom we have information – Fisherman, Farmer, and the Scheduled Caste – the husband's family brings food gifts (*(y)ecca*) to the girl's natal home around one month after the birth occurs. These are the makings for a meal, including spices, rice, butter, and betel- areca; at this time they are called 'new mother spices' (*baaNanti–kaara*). Our Farmer caste informant told us that the new mother also carries *dose* and some other snacks and vegetable preparations with her when she finally returns to her marital home with her baby two or three months later. This person mentioned a snack called *tamTa*, uncooked balls made of a ground-up mixture of **jaggery, dry coconut (*kobbari*), Bengal gram (roasted), sesame, cardamom, and ginger.** As many of these ingredients appear in other rituals, this preparation may possibly have some symbolic value.

Summary: Plants in Seventh Month Pregnancy Rituals

This is a relatively simple rite of passage, but an important one nonetheless, especially in terms of the developing relationship between two families united by a marriage. Some of the rituals that celebrate pregnancy – such as putting on bangles or 'lap filling', and 'putting rice' – are reminiscent of girls' maturation ceremonies and rites associated with marriage. Rubbing the cheeks with turmeric and oil, filling the lap with good things (plantains, rice, coconuts, betel-areca), in luck numbers (such as 5) – these are familiar from other auspicious rites of passage. A few details, however, seem unique to this occasion. The use of fig-leaf buds in the Iyengar Brahman ritual seems to be an especially striking allusion to the newly forming person about to be born. Another interesting detail is the Smartha Brahman use of a coconut with its husk on it. It is a ripe coconut (reference the almost-formed human baby?), but still inside its container (the womb?). Another noteworthy detail is in the Farmer caste 'lap-filling' ritual, which includes rice paddy, rather than husked rice. This element seems particularly suitable to a situation in which the unborn baby is not yet ready for life in human society. Though we do not have much information on whether other castes' also use rice paddy in this way, there is ample use of a winnowing fan (*moRa*) in birth rituals, further highlighting the husking process.[71] Plant materials used in these pregnancy rituals are summarized below in Table 6.

---

[71] It is worth mentioning in this context that there are ceremonies for the threshing floor performed annually. And various customs associated with threshing grain. For example, we were told that non-Brahman woman should have some tattoos on their forearms before they winnow grain.

Table 6. Plant Materials Used in Seventh Month Pregnancy Rituals

Botanical Name	Kannada Name	Uses
Cicer arietinum Bengal gram	*huri kaDale* -roasted gram	-An ingredient of the *tamTa* snack carried by the new mother returning to her husband's family (Farmer)
Cocos nucifera Coconut	*tengin kaayi* - ripe coconut	Ripe coconut: Used in lap-filling ceremony Used with outer covering still on (Smartha Brahman)
	kobbari - dried coconut	-Dried coconut: An ingredient of the *tamTa* snack carried by the new mother returning to her husband's family (Farmer)
Curcuma longa Turmeric	*arasiNa*	-Mixed with oil, rubbed on cheeks of the pregnant woman, at the beginning of the ritual (Smith Caste) -Turmeric-colored rice (*akšate*) used to bless the husband and wife

Table 6. Plant Materials Used in Seventh Month Pregnancy Rituals

Botanical Name	Kannada Name	Uses
Ficus indica Banyan	*aala chigaru* - leaf bud	Fluid from combination of three types of mashed-up buds put in nostrils of pregnant woman (Iyengar Brahman)
Ficus religiosa Pipal	*araLi chigaru* - leaf bud	
Ficus glomerata Country fig	*atti chigaru* - leaf bud	
Musa sapientum Plantain	*baaLe haNNu* - ripe plantain	Used in 'lap-filling' ritual
Oryza sativa Rice	*bhatta* - rice paddy *akki* - raw rice	Used in 'lap-filling' ritual (paddy and/or raw rice) Used in 'rice putting' ritual (raw rice)
Piper betle Betel	*viLyadele* - betel leaves	-Tied-up packet of leaves given to pregnant woman in the 'lap-filling' ritual (Farmer)
Sesamum indicum Sesame	*puTTeLLu* - sesame seeds	-An ingredient of the *tamTa* snack carried by the new mother when she returns to her husband's family home (Farmer)

Rituals Associated with Death and Widowhood

Funerary rites, as the ultimate "inauspicious" occasions, differ in some important ways from the life-celebrating rituals discussed thus far. The clear purpose is to help the soul of the deceased to go to *swaraga* 'heaven' – to be sure that he or she is at peace, fully satisfied, not likely to come back and cause trouble as a ghost. Marriage represents the fulfillment of a person's journey through life. Thus, if a boy or man dies before marrying, all or most of the non-Brahman castes perform some kind of wedding for him before the next family marriage. Otherwise, males and females receive the same funeral rites in almost all groups. If a man pre-deceases his wife, her widowhood status is established by some specific funeral rites. Most non-Brahman and Scheduled Caste groups bury their dead in this region. Brahmans, on the other hand, cremate them, unless they are very young children, in which case they bury them.

The number "1" and even numbers (especially 2 and 4) are customary parts of funerary rituals. For example, four people carry a body to the grave, we were told, never five or seven or any other auspicious (odd) number. Even if the body is driven in a car, this person continued, there will be four people in the car escorting him or her. A man of the Smith caste told me that on the day someone dies, it is customary to put one betel leaf, one areca nut, one strand of *darbhe* grass (*Poa cynosuroides*),[72] and a one-rupee or a one-*paise* coin on a plate on the body." One is never used for an auspicious event," he explained.

---

[72] An Iyengar Brahman informant told me that a two-strand ring of this same grass is put on the finger of a deceased person before cremation. A *darbhe* grass ring, he continued, is also used on auspicious occasions, but in other numbers, such as three.

While the body is in the house, he continued, a small plate of **raw rice** with a small sickle (*kuDugoolu*) is set on it, to be sure that the person does not become a ghost (*pichaachi*).

A death, like a birth, creates a ten-day state of ritual pollution (*sutaka*) for the patrilineal kin group. Others will not take food from the family during this time; and the family home is carefully purified (whitewashed, the floor smeared with cow dung, clay pots replaced, other utensils washed) when the ten days is over. Eleventh-day *tithi* rituals mark the end of the period of ritual pollution.

Our information on death-related rituals comes from in-depth interviews with members of 11 different castes and subcastes[73] and observations of funerals of three different castes.[74]

Among Brahmans, it is customary to observe one's parents' or other close relatives' death anniversaries, also called *tithi*. Non-Brahmans may conduct rituals on the first anniversary after a death; but after the first year they revere their dead in the Pitra Paksha (*Malada-habba*) festival for ancestors, to be described briefly below.[75]

The Scheduled Caste community in Bandipur Village during the period of this research had the right and responsibility to provide services as *kuluvadis*. This job was inherited patrilineally. It earned them a small government stipend and some land. The assigned *kuluvadi* duties, which rotated monthly within the community, were grave-digging, building wedding canopies, serving visiting officials, and arresting people who did not pay their taxes.

---

[73] Scheduled Caste, Smith, Washerman, Barber, Fisherman, Oil Presser, Iyengar Brahman, Smartha Brahman, and three Farmer subcastes (Daas, Mull, and Jogi Okkaligas).

[74] Fisherman, Oil Presser, and Farmer.

[75] My book, *Coloured Rice*, has a detailed discussion of this event.

As with other rites of passage, funerals require some specific plants and plant materials. These differ in interesting ways from those used in other rites of passage.

The day of a death

When someone dies, all castes for which we have information bathe the corpse in hot water, put clean clothes on the body, and decorate and offer *puja* worship to it. In one Oil Presser home we observed the following process after a middle-aged man had died. His wife survived him, so her transition to widowhood was part of the funeral:

> The family sends out word of the death to various relatives.[76] The relatives tell us, "Monday is a good day to die, so his soul is at rest. His life is completely finished." Caste-mates all bring plates containing two **plantains, betel nuts**, and **turmeric** with vermillion.
>
> A garland of three kinds of flowers/plants is made for him to wear: *Ocymum sanctum* (*tuLasi*), *Solanum nigrum* (*gaaNike huuvu*), and **jasmine** (*kaakaDa huuvu*). His body is bathed in warm water and dried with a towel. A new white cloth is put over him. A towel is wrapped on his head as a turban, *vibhuti* is put on his forehead,[77] and the garland is put on him. (An Oil Presser man told me

---

[76] Carrying these messages can be a task assigned to *kuluvadis*.

[77] This is a Saivite custom. Vaishnavite families put the *naama* image on the forehead.

that hibiscus (*dasavalahuuvu*) is required for such a garland.)

A woman prepares some **betel-areca** for him, and pieces of **sandalwood** are put on a plate and burned in front of his body, which is now ready for viewing.

The dead man's wife, dressed in a new sari, sits next to him. Her mother rubs a large quantity of **turmeric** and oil on her chin and cheeks, *davaNa* (a fragrant white flower)[78] in her hair, and vermillion on her forehead. Her mother puts a garland on her and does *aarathi* for her with a plate of red liquid.

Caste-mates and other friends and neighbors come to wave incense sticks, as a gesture of respect for the deceased man. One man touches the dead man's feet and bows to him, and his wife puts rice on the widow's head, flowers in her hair, and another garland on her neck.

The widow does incense-stick *puja* to her deceased husband and puts some **betel-areca** into his hand.

All items used in this phase of the ceremony are bundled into a towel, which will be given to members of the Scheduled Caste later on.

This sequence is generally similar to that of other castes. In the Mull Okkaliga Farmer subcaste, we were told that soon after a death

---

[78] Information on flower color from Helen Ullrich (personal communication).

a plate is put onto the deceased person. It contains **raw rice, jaggery, sesame seeds, areca nuts,** and one sickle. An informant from this group told us that villagers also come bringing **raw rice,** some of which they throw on the head of the deceased person, putting the rest on the plate set on his or her chest.

The Barber caste custom is to break a **coconut** before offering *puja* to the corpse. A Washerman caste woman told us that the ashes used to heat the fire for the corpse's bath are placed into an empty pot and later dumped "somewhere out in the fields."

A Smartha Brahman informant told us that the family will light a fire in front of the house when an adult dies, and a priest (*joyish*) will come. The dead person's sons will go to the river with new clothes on and take a bath in the river. They carry water back from the river: this will be used to bathe the corpse. (If the river is too far away, the corpse may be bathed at the riverside.) All relatives put raw **rice** (*akki*) into the mouth of the deceased person.[79]

Figure 27. Widow Seated to the Left of Her Deceased Husband. Oil Presser caste funeral, Bandipur, 1966

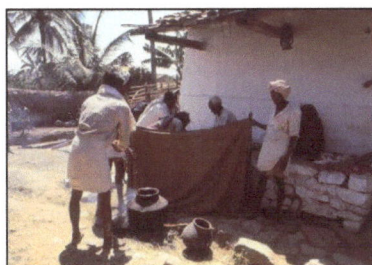

Figure 28. Washing the Corpse Before the Public Viewing. Oil Presser caste, Bandipur, 1966

[79] According to Helen Ullrich (personal communication), raw rice is used for this purpose. The ritual act is called *akki haakta* 'putting raw rice'.

Figure 29. A Nephew of the Deceased Man Cries Loudly, as friends and relatives offer *puja*: Fisherman caste, Bandipur, 1966

Figure 30. A Caste-mate Offers a Final Incense-stick *puja* to the Deceased Man: Fisherman caste, Bandipur, 1966

Going to the burial or cremation place

The corpse is carried to the grave or cremation place on a wooden stretcher (*cheTTa* or *kurju*) by four men, accompanied by close patrilineal relatives (*dayaadi*). Among most non-Brahmans and the Scheduled Caste, it is customary for the group to sprinkle "puffed" **Bengal gram** (*kaDale puri*) on the body and the path as they move along.

Our observation notes describe an Oil Presser caste funeral procession:

> A brass plate with a piece of **jaggery**, some **raw rice**, and an iron knife is kept on the chest of the deceased man, under the white cloth that covers him. On each corner of the stretcher is one **plantain** and one **betel-areca** set, taken from his wife's sari. His daughter carries some fire.

The group stops along the path, and the pall-bearers set down the stretcher. The two men at the front change places with those at the rear. A man digs a hole in the path near the corpse's head, puts some **betel-areca** into the hole, and covers it up.

The same procedure was followed in the Fisherman caste funeral we observed, but this group set a small *Leucas indica* plant (Figures 32 and 33) on top of the hole with **betel-areca** in it. Someone explained to us that this is done because "the ghost cannot cross the spot where this stop was made; he cannot come back to the village."

Among Smartha Brahmans, the eldest son of the deceased person leads the procession to the cremation place. He carries some fire in a pot. They do not sprinkle puffed Bengal gram on the path.

Burial, cremation, and widowhood rituals

Brahmans will have built a funeral pyre near the river. The Iyengars told us that any "**wild sticks**," in alternating layers with cow dung cakes, could be used, but our Smartha Brahman informant told us that it should be built with **sandalwood** and cow dung cakes:

The corpse is put on top of the funeral pyre. He/She is naked, except that a man's sacred thread is kept on. A copper or gold coin may be in his/her mouth. The body's private parts are covered with a **plantain leaf**.

The priest chants mantras, as the eldest son of the deceased person lights the fire with a torch carried from the home. The second, third, and other sons also put flames to the fire in birth order.

The sons' heads are shaved, in hierarchical order, and they bathe in the river. They should stay until the corpse is fully burned. When the corpse's head bursts,[80] all those who touched it must bathe, change their sacred threads, and put on newly-washed clothes.

Non-Brahman and Scheduled Caste families' rituals performed at the grave-site are called by some *guddu puja*, meaning 'grave-side worship'.[81] They may use a priest (Brahman or non- Brahman), and the grave is oriented north-south. In the Oil Presser funeral we observed, the group carried the corpse on its stretcher twice clockwise around the grave before burial. The Fisherman group did it three times; and three was also said to be the custom of the Mull Okkaliga Farmers.

All of the non-Brahman and Scheduled Caste groups for whom we have information, except the Smiths, set a *Leucas indica* (Kannada, *tumbe giDa*) plant at the head-end of the grave after the body has been buried. Other plants also were used in the Fisherman caste funeral we observed:

One **plantain leaf** and some *Cassia fistula* leaves (Kannada, *kakke soppu*) were set into the empty grave before the corpse was put into it. All decorations (flowers, jewel

---

[80] William Crooke (1909:468) mentions a common belief that the soul resides in the head, and that of a virtuous person leaves from the head.

[81] K. Gurulingaiah notes, 1967. An alternative term, *gudli puja*, is mentioned by Helen Ullrich for Shimoga District. (personal communication)

necklace) and clothing were removed from the body, and a small piece of gold was put into his mouth. The torso of the body was covered with one **plantain leaf** and some *Cassia fistula* (Kannada, *kakke*). A new, white cloth (a *panche* or *lungi*) was put on top of him. His head was at the south end of the grave.

Figure 31. Mourners Bathing at the River after the Burial.
Fisherman caste funeral, Bandipur

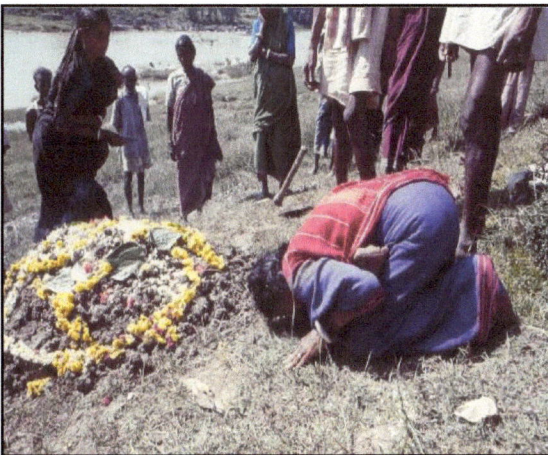

Figure 32. Woman Prostrating to the Grave.
Fisherman caste funeral, Bandipur

107

Figure 33. *Leucas indica* Plant (source: https://commons.wikim edia.org/wiki/File: Leucas_aspera_plant.jpg#/media/File:a Leucas_aspera_plant.jpg)

Figure 34. Procession to the Grave. Fisherman caste funeral, Bandipur

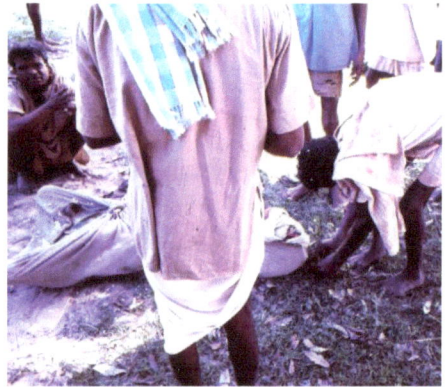

Figure 35. Setting a *Leucas indica* Plant in the Path to the Grave(Bandipur, Oil Presser funeral)

Relatives, caste-mates, and friends (two brothers of the deceased, his son's daughters husband, a local caste-mate, and a Muslim friend) each threw three handfuls of earth onto the body, covering the head first. Someone explained to us that, "Mud should be thrown in only from the right or left sides, never put under the legs." A pile of salt was put onto the stomach.

The grave was filled with earth by *kuluvadis*. All garlands, flowers, **betel-areca, ripe plantains**, and some coins, and **turmeric**-vermillion were put on top of the grave. Some *tuLasi* leaves (*Ocymum sanctum*) and a small stone were put at the head-end of the grave.[82]

Several men and women prostrated to the grave, one-by-one, touching their heads to the small stone, as a band-set played music. After this *puja*, some broken **coconut** pieces were placed on top of the flowers and other items.

Everyone present went to the river to bathe, and we all had water with cow dung sprinkled on our heads. **Betel-areca** was distributed. The deceased man's nephew rinsed all cloth items in the river, intending to do worship for them after returning to the house.

The Oil Presser burial we observed was generally similar, with the addition of a *Leucas indica* plant set together with a *tuLasi* **twig** at the head of the grave, and the face of the deceased also covered with a **plantain leaf.** Water from a broken **coconut** was sprinkled around the foot area of the grave in a counter-clockwise motion; and the coconut was set at the foot of the grave.

This funeral included the

---

[82] Our notes on this event do not mention placing the *Leucas indica* twig on this grave, but it is most likely that this was done.

Transition of a 'married woman' (*muTTayide*) to the status of widow:

> After she had prostrated to the grave, the wife of the deceased man sat as her mother broke some of the glass bangles from her hands, scattering the pieces over the head of the grave.

> The wife patted her own mouth repeatedly, as her mother wiped the **turmeric** and oil off of her cheeks. (The other women present became angry, because the mother started doing this without telling them in advance. It was wrong for them to see this, they said.)

After returning to the house, we watched as people in the Fisherman family touched some **tamarind**-water, to purify themselves. Next, the son of the deceased man held a winnowing fan with some **raw rice** and two **betel leaves** in it over his head. With his back to the house, he threw the contents of the winnowing fan onto the roof of the house.

Rituals performed soon after a death

The patrilineal group remains in a state of 'ritual pollution' *(sutaka)* for ten days after a death. But certain ceremonies still are performed during this period. Non-Brahmans and the Scheduled Caste people we interviewed perform a ceremony on the fifth day after a death. This is called *chakrašanti* by most groups.

Among Smartha Brahmans, the same men who attended the cremation do a ceremony called *asti sanchayana*, 'collecting the bones', on the second day after a death:

> They bring with them a **tender coconut**,[83] some **raw rice, green gram**, cow dung cakes, and a cooking pot to the cremation place. All of the men bathe in the river before collecting the ashes.

> They pour five or six pitchers of water on the bed of ashes, to cool any burning embers; and they collect all ashes, immersing them in the river (or a tank or well), leaving only the bones of the deceased.

> As the bones are gathered, the priest names each one ('collar bone', 'limb', etc.), and they are put into a new clay pot. The eldest son of the deceased carries this pot behind him and immerses it in the river without ever looking at it. ("He should not see it," we were told.) The sons all bathe and then do another ritual, called *bhumitaayi šanti* 'mother earth peace'. [notes unavailable].

> The **tender coconut** is opened "from the eye side, which is an 'inauspicious act' done only on this occasion." It is then inverted at the cremation place, so the liquid runs out.

> The sons take another bath and cook the preparation, called *bhuTabaLi* 'ghost food', with rice and **green gram**.

---

[83] If a child over age five has died and been cremated, they also bring some **coconut flowers** (*hombaaLe*).

Among non-Brahmans and the Scheduled Caste, the fifth day after a death is the occasion of a ritual called *chakrasanti*. These rituals are completed out in the fields under a tree. A leaf shed is built, and a meal (*(y)eDe*) is offered. A Scheduled Caste informant of the Daas sect described their community's rituals to us:[84]

The eldest son of the deceased shaves his head. Inside the leaf shed are set four mounds of wet mud, which are called 'pots'. Each mound has on top of it some **sacred fig leaves** and small lamps.

[Food is cooked outdoors.] Specific requirements for this meal are: *kaaysoppin saaru,* finger millet balls (*raagi hiTTu*), cooked rice, meat, *citrann/ huranna, dose, vaDe, chakkali,* and **puffed Bengal gram.** With guidance from a *Daasayya,* a meal is set in front of the leaf shed and offered to the 'pots' as *(y)eDe.* The meal that was offered to the 'pots' is eaten by the man whose head is shaved.

The Jogi Okkaliga subcaste of Farmers described their fifth day ceremony to us:

One son of the deceased has had his head shaved. (Eldest son, for the father; youngest, for the mother).

---

[84] Members of the Mull (Saivite) sect in this caste do the same ritual, but only on the 11th day after a death. The person who explained this to us said that Daas families tend to do this offering and conclude the mourning period then and there, instead of doing the 11th day ceremony, because it is so expensive.

Food (both vegetarian and non-vegetarian) is cooked outdoors, under a **banyan tree**. Five mounds of clay, called *kamba* 'pots', are set in a circle, with one new clay pot full of water (called *kandalu*) in the center.

The ritual is called 'four *kaLashas* and one pot' (*naalku kamba, ondu kumbu*): A thread is wrapped nine times around all the pots, and an oil-lamp is set together with a wheel made out of ***Securinega leucopyrus (huLikaDDi/ huLukaDDi)*** in front of them. They set out two meals, offered as *(y)eDe*, and break **five coconuts**.

Next is a *shaastra* called *tale koLLi hiDiyuvudu*. The pot filled with water is put on the right shoulder of the son whose head has been shaved. He turns around five times as he holds the pot. Every time he turns around, the priest (*Aynoru*) pecks the pot with a sickle, making a hole in it. On the fifth round, the son shatters the pot on a stone that has been set near the *kambas*.

After the pot has been broken, everyone cries for a while. Then they put out the fire of a burning torch in the water that has spilled out; and everyone eats a meal. Of the two specially offered meals, one is eaten by the son with the shaved head. The other can be eaten by anyone else. Any food remaining from the meal is left in the fields, not taken back to the house.

113

Rituals on the 11th day, concluding the period of ritual pollution

Sutaka pollution is removed at the end of the ten-day period by whitewashing the house, rubbing the floors with cow dung and water (or cow urine), replacing clay pots, and cleaning all vessels. Affected family members are expected to bathe. Men of the "twice-born" castes change their sacred threads.

The Fisherman caste ritual we observed took place outside, under a tree, not at or near the grave-site. The son of the deceased man had his head shaved in the afternoon. They performed the *chakrasanti* ritual, much in the way the Jogi Okkaligas did for their fifth-day ritual, adding other actions, to conclude the period of ritual pollution. A small shrine (*chapra*) was constructed with wood branches at the base of the tree. inside the shrine was a **tender coconut** with a hole in its top, placed on a small mud platform. A bunch of **coconut flowers** was inserted into the hole at the top of the coconut. Two mud mounds (*kumba*) also were inside the shrine. Other offerings were: **yellow chrysanthemums**, a **betel-areca** set, two *biiDi* cigarettes, some snacks (*chekli, vaDe*), and some **puffed Bengal gram.** It was decorated with **mango leaves** and some others (including *baine(y)ele*, a type of palm tree).[85]

A trusted priest (*Aynoru*)[86] from a neighboring village was officiating. He sprinkled water on the ground under the

---

[85] Information from Malla Setty. Botanical identification not available.
[86] A brief interview with this man is in Annex-2.

shrine and set a brass image of the Thirupathi God, Venkatarama swamy, inside.

Four mud mounds (called *kamba*, 'pots') were arranged in a circle in front of the shrine with a clay pot (*chembu*) filled with water in the center. Each of the four 'pots' had next to it one **betel leaf** with one **ripe plantain** on it, and a coin worth one *paise* on the plantain. A fifth set was added on the edge of the arrangement, for the *chembu*. A very long string was tied around all the 'pots'.

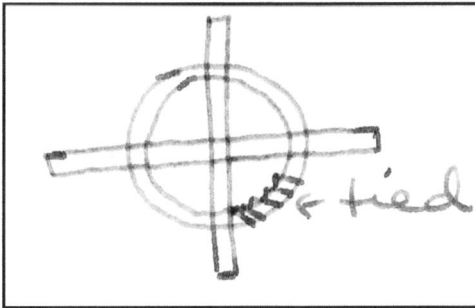

Figure 36. *Chakra* Made by Aynoru Priest
(diagram from author's field notes)

The priest had made a *"chakra"* with two crossed sticks of **Nerium indicum** (*kanugul kaDDi*) tied cross-wise with a special thread. He stuck fresh **lime fruits** onto the points of the *chakra*. (Figure 36)

A mixture of finely ground **cumin** and **sesame** was put into the *chembu* by a male relative.

The priest put vermillion and flowers on each of the four *kumbas* and into the mouth of the small water pot

115

(*chembu*). He then put vermillion on the chest of a male relative (the deceased man's son's wife's elder brother), then onto the *taaLi* of the deceased man's son's wife, and finally on the foreheads of everyone else.

After some more worship for God and for the 'pots', a ritual 'body washing' took place: the four men who had carried the body to the grave sat facing away from the shrine, and the priest put water on their shoulders.

Someone blew a conch shell horn as the son of the deceased, his shirt now off, put a burning log on the strings surrounding the 'pots'. The priest then knocked over the four 'pots', and the son walked clockwise around the space holding the small pot of water (*chembu*) at the back of his neck.

The priest then hit the water pot with a stick, so the water ran down the son's back, and the son threw it down onto the space where it had sat, shattering it completely as he made a whooping noise, clapping his hand over his mouth. He then threw the clay shards and the remaining mud 'pots' into the river. The priest poured warm water over the son, who put on a clean *panche/lungi* (man's waist-cloth).

Concluding the rite, the priest put two **plantain leaves** inside the shrine, saying "One meal for God and one for Narsayya [the deceased man]." On each leaf was a large meal, with fish, chicken, vegetables, one egg, two coconuts, and other items, including 14 **plantains** and a bunch of **grapes**. A bell rang as a coconut was broken. The close relatives offered worship to the food. Everyone chanted "Govinda" over and over, meaning that the deceased man now has left this world and gone to *swaraga* (heaven).

Other non-Brahman castes' concluding rituals seem to be done mostly at home, not outdoors. Having the eldest son shave his head and offering a meal to the deceased are more or less universal. Many will offer things that the deceased person especially liked. A *daasayya* may blow a conch shell horn. It is assumed that close relatives and other caste-mates also will be feasted on this occasion in the best way that the family can afford (*i.e.,* serving meat, or at least chicken, for the non-vegetarians). The Jogi Okkaligas' custom is to go to the grave on the 11th day and pour some milk and clarified butter on it before food is offered, along with clothes and favored items, to the deceased person inside the house.

The Smith caste custom is to keep a small vessel (*kaLasha*) "in the name of the departed person," setting it near to their belongings along with some cooked food on three **plantain leaves**. For the meal on this day a stir-fry preparation (*palya*) made with **unripe plantains** is "compulsory" in this community. After being offered to the deceased person (in the form of the *kaLasha*) and worshipped, some of the food is carried to the river, where it is immersed, before food is served to caste-mates.

Brahmans' customs also include sons' (and perhaps some patrilineal cousins) shaving their heads and the feeding of close relatives; and men's sacred threads are changed on the 11th day. On the tenth day (*dashooha*) after a death, Smartha Brahman sons and sons-in-law of the deceased gather at the riverside and cook rice over a cow dung fire after having a river bath. This rice preparation is called *bhuTabali* (lit. 'ghost food'). After they return to the house, they must eat the preparation called *uddinavaDe*, which is made with **black gram**. On the 11th day, the family is expected to serve food to all members of their patrilineage (*dayaadi*). Iyengar Brahmans set a food offering at the cremation place on the 10th day after a death, along with a **tender coconut** and **coconut flowers**.

It is customary for both Iyengar and Smartha Brahmans to feed a group of Brahmans on the 12th day after a death – 16 men (=4x4) in the Iyengar case. There are some special Brahmans who provide this service. They are called "12th Day Brahmans." They tend to be poor men, and they are regarded as low status. We were told that, if a Smartha family cannot afford the services of the 12th Day Brahmans, the mourners could go to the riverside and cook the same foods, setting them out as *(y)eDe* offerings on three **plantain leaf** plates while a priest chants mantras. These three meals are buried in a ditch. Next, three *pinDa* balls are made with **cooked rice**, honey, curds, and **sesame seeds**. These *pinDa* balls are named. One is divided into two parts and set out as an offering, with the meaning that, "The departed soul joins with ancestors, becomes a *pitaamaha*." All utensils used for this cooking are given to the priest. All participants (*kartrus*, all males) bathe and change their sacred threads. When they return to their house, they look at their reflections in oil. (During the mourning period, they should not have seen their own reflections in any mirror;

nor should they have put any marks on their foreheads until the 12th day.)

Our Iyengar informant told us that if 16 "12th Day Brahmans" could not be found, then 16 **plantain leaves** with rice, vegetables, and other items (<u>no</u> **coconuts**) would be given to a temple. At least four Brahmans, he said, would actually come for a meal. Each one would receive a pair of *panches/lungis,* a silver cup (if the family can afford it), and two rupees. Other gifts distributed to them may include a bed with a pillow, a carpet, blanket, walking stick, a bell-metal plate with curds and rice, and one iron sickle. After feeding the four Brahmans and making such presentations to them, our informant told us, the family would invite caste-mates for a meal.

Rituals for deceased children

The rituals described thus far all relate to deaths of adults, who presumably have completed much of their life's work. All castes have special, simplified ways of managing the sad deaths of "children," including those who may be mature but have not yet married (or had their sacred thread ceremonies, among the "twice born"). No *(y)eDe* foods are offered; nor are there many special *shaastras* on the day of such a death. These rituals mostly do not include interesting botanical items; but they deserve attention, to complete this report on rites of passage.

As mentioned earlier, all non-Brahman and Scheduled Caste families perform some kind of "marriage" (*iragana maduve*) on the occasion of the next family wedding, if one of their male (not female) children happens to have died before his marriage, especially if they are more than three or five years old. We were told that the "marriage" could be performed between a cow and a bull (Washerman informant), between two vessels (*kaLashas*) or two distantly related boys/girls (Fisherman, Daas Okkaliga)[87], or between the boy's spirit and a **sacred fig tree** or a cow, or between **two piles of flowers** (Mull Okkaliga), depending on what the priest recommends. One Daas Okkaliga (Farmer caste) informant told us that, "A bunch of flowers may be put around a *kaLasha* vessel for a boy who has died. On top of the vessel is a **coconut**. A *taaLi* is tied to that vessel. On that day, the boy goes to *swaraga*." This 'mock marriage' ritual, we were told by a Farmer caste family, gives the spirit of a deceased boy some "peace."

Among Brahmans, very young children (under age 5) are buried, not cremated. Milk and clarified butter is poured on their graves by both Smarthas and Iyengars. Among Smartha Brahmans, a 'mock *upanayana*' (sacred thread ceremony) is done for a boy who dies before his initiation ceremonies, but no 11th day *tithi* is done for him. If a child over age five dies in this caste, a **tender coconut,** some **coconut flowers,** and some **cooked rice with green gram** (but <u>no</u> **turmeric**) are set on the cremation place on the day after cremation. The tender coconut is inverted, and the liquid runs out. Our Iyengar informants told us that milk and clarified butter are poured at a child's cremation place before the collection of bones, which are then spread on water. On the tenth day after a child's death, a special combination of foods, called *(y)eriappa,*[88] is put on the cremation place, along with a **tender coconut** and **coconut flowers.** Caste-mates are not invited to a meal.

---

[87] A Jogi Okkaliga (Farmer) informant told us that they formerly had a girl and a boy do this ritual, "but the girls who acted as brides in this ceremony did not prosper, so we now avoid involving actual girls."

[88] This is a combination of snack foods, including *vaDe, tenkoLalu* (a fried snack), *sikkionDe* (a deep-fried sweet), and *raviunDe.* (The term *(y)eriappa* also refers to a fried preparation made with soaked raw rice, jaggery, and coconut, according

Four days of *tithi* rituals are done for a initiated boy who dies, starting on the ninth day after his death. The family is 'polluted', but they do not invite others for meals after the pollution period ends, as they would do in the case of an adult's death.

Summary: Plants and Plant Parts in Death Rituals

Table 6 summarizes our information on plant materials customarily used in death rituals. Most of the plant materials used in funerary rituals are familiar from other rites of passage, but they may appear in different ways. For example, Bengal gram, seen in many other settings as a soaked or plain food item, now appears in its "puffed" form. *Leucas indica* was used as a flower in other rites of passage, but in funerals it appears as a more or less whole plant, a twig with leaves (and possibly also flowers), a *giDa* to be "planted" on a grave. A truly distinctive plant item in funerary rituals is the coconut flower. It looks much like the areca flower and is called by the same name, *hombaaLe*, but, as far as we know, it is not used on "auspicious" occasions in this region of Karnataka. Puncturing a coconut at the "eye end" (said to be an ominous/inauspicious act) and having the liquid drain out, as some groups do, is an apt metaphor for the loss of life. Betel-areca sets or plantains, found in virtually all other rituals, appear in some funeral rites only one at a time, expressing inauspicious numbers such as "one" or "four."

There may be more emphasis on cooked food in funerals, or on cooking as part of the ritual, than in other rites of passage, although there are plenty of festive meals served on all occasions.

---

to Helen Ullrich, personal communication.)

This may possibly reflect a belief that the dead person might be hungry, and a wish to satisfy any possible hunger to ensure a peaceful and contented progress of the soul on to *swaraga*.[89] At least one caste, the Smiths, requires a preparation of **unripe plantains** in the meal for the 11th day *tithi*. These do not seem to be required by any group whatsoever on auspicious occasions.

In the case of widows, their flowers, glass bangles, and turmeric - - all emblems of the much- celebrated "married woman" status -- are removed once a husband has been buried. This loss is a tragedy that most women fear. (Further information on the widowhood transition is in Annex 3. Information on plant materials in death rituals is summarized below in Table 7.

---

[89] In Bandipur Village I knew a family whose elderly mother was dying. She was staying on the verandah of the house, so that when she died, her ghost would not go into the rafters of the house and cause problems. Her daughter told me that, "When she dies we will offer her very good food, so she will be satisfied."

Table 7. Plant Materials Used in Death Rituals

Botanical Name	Kannada Name	Uses (*=widespread)
	Mixture Raw rice Jaggery Sesame seeds Areca nuts	On a plate set onto the chest of a body being carried to the grave (Mull Okkaliga)
	Mixture One ripe plantain One betel-areca set	At the corners of the stretcher carrying a body to the grave (Oil Presser)
	Mixture One piece of jaggery Raw rice Iron knife	Plate on chest of dead man being carried to the grave (Oil Presser)
	Combination of cooked foods called *(y)eriappa:* *-vaDe* *-tenkoLalu* *-sikkionunDe* *-raviunDe*	Offered by Iyengars along with tender coconut and coconut flowers, at cremation place, 10th day after a child's death.
Areca catchu	*aDike*	-Set on a plate on the chest of a deceased person, along with jaggery, sesame seeds, and raw rice (Mull Okkaliga) -Offered as part of betel-areca set at certain points in the ceremony. -Betel-areca set buried at spot on the path to the grave, where *Leucas indica* plant is set, to prevent return of the ghost to the village. (*)

Table 7. Plant Materials Used in Death Rituals

Botanical Name	Kannada Name	Uses (*=widespread)
Cassia fistula	*kakke -soppu* 'leaf	Put in the grave, beneath and on top of the corpse, with *tuLasi* (Fisherman caste)
Chrysanthemum spp. [chrysanthemum]	*savantigehuuvu* 'flower'	Often used for garlands, yellow color (*) Set onto grave, yellow color (Fisherman caste funeral)
Cicer arietinum [Bengal gram]	*kaDale-puri* 'puffed'	Sprinkled on a corpse and on the path to the grave-site (*) Offered in small shrine at the conclusion of the 'pollution' period (Fisherman)
Cocos nucifera [coconut]	*tengin kaayi* 'ripe coconut'	Ripe coconut broken before doing *puja* to a corpse, on the day of death (Barber)
	hombaaLe 'coconut flower'	Broken coconut set on top of grave. Coconut Flowers are used in various ceremonies after a death, including 11th day *tithi*(*)
		Liquid from inverted tender coconut spilled onto the foot-end of a grave (Oil Presser), or on the cremation place (Smartha Brahman), or on the grave of a child (Smartha) Coconuts offered in 5th- day ceremony under a banyan tree (Jogi Okkaliga) Tender coconut in *(y)eDe* meal 10th day after Iyengar Brahman child's death
	(y)eleniiru 'tender coconut'	Coconuts are not given to the temple as 12th-Day offerings by Iyengar Brahmans.

Table 7. Plant Materials Used in Death Rituals

Botanical Name	Kannada Name	Uses (*=widespread)
Cuminum cyminium [cumin]	*jiirige*	Finely ground and mixed with sesame, used in Fisherman caste 11th day ceremony.
Curcuma longa [turmeric]	*arasiNa*	Rubbed with oil on the widow's cheeks before her husband's burial, and wiped off at his grave. Mixture of turmeric and vermillion sprinkled on top of a grave (*) Excluded from green gram preparation in meal after a young child's death (Smartha Brahman)
Ficus indica [banyan]	*aaladamara*	Food cooked outdoors, under a banyan tree, for 5th day ceremony (Jogi Okkaliga)
Ficus religiosa [sacred fig]	*araLimara*	Leaves used in outdoor ceremony, on 5th day after a death (Scheduled Caste)
Hibiscus spp.	*daasavaaLahuuvu*	Preferred for funeral garland (Oil Presser verbal report)
Jasminium spp.	*kaakaDahuuvu malligehuuvu*	Used in funerary garland, along with *Ocymum sanctum* and *Solanum nigrum* flowers (Oil Presser)
Leucas indica	*tumbe* -*giDa* 'twig'	"Planted" at head end of a grave (*) and/or on the path to the grave-site
Mangifera indica [mango]	*maavin - soppu* 'leaf'	Used to decorate shrine under a tree, in 11th-day *tithi* (Fisherman)
Musa sapientum [plantain]	*baaLe -(y)ele* 'leaf' *baaLe-kaayi* 'unripe/green plantain'	Leaf used to cover a corpse's torso (and face) during burial or cremation(*) Unripe plantain a required food in some funeral feasts (Smith)

125

Table 7. Plant Materials Used in Death Rituals

Botanical Name	Kannada Name	Uses (*=widespread)
Nerium indicum [oleander]	wood: *kaNigal-kaDDi*	Used to make a "*chakra*" by a ritual specialist in 11th day ceremony, after Fisherman caste funeral
Ocymum sanctum [sacred basil]	*tuLasi - soppu* 'leaf'	Leaf put in the grave, beneath and on top of the corpse, with *Leucas indica* (Fisherman caste) Used in funeral garland (Oil-Presser caste) Twig set at head of the grave together with *Leucas indica* (Oil-Presser caste)
Oryzva sativa [rice]	*akki* 'raw rice'	Raw rice put into the mouth of a deceased person by relatives before cremation (Smartha Brahman) Rice set onto a plate for the deceased, and thrown on his/her head by caste- mates (non-Brahmans, Scheduled Caste)(*)
Phaseolus aureus [green gram]	*hesaru kaaLu* 'whole gram'	Cooked outdoors after the 'collection of ashes' (Smartha Brahman)
Piper betle [betel]	*viLLadele* 'leaf'	Betel-areca put into hand of the deceased person(*) Betel-areca set buried on the path to the burial place (*)
Poa cynosuroides	*darbhe/darbha* grass	A single blade of grass put on plate for the deceased person (Smith caste) Two-strand ring put on finger of a corpse before cremation (Iyengar)
Saccharum	*bella* 'jaggery'	Set onto a plate for a newly deceased person, together with sesame, raw rice, and areca nuts(*)

Table 7. Plant Materials Used in Death Rituals

Botanical Name	Kannada Name	Uses (*=widespread)
Santalum album	*srigandha*	Pieces of sandalwood burned on a plate before the newly washed body, before public viewing (Oil Presser)
Securinega leucopyrus	*hulikaDDi/huLu-kaDDi*	Branch or stick used in Jogi Okkaliga 5th day ceremony
Sesamum indicum [sesame]	*puTeLLu*	-Put on plate for corpse (with other items), on the day of death (Mull Okkaliga) -Used in Fisherman caste 11th day ritual -One ingredient of *pinDa* balls, in 10th day ceremony (Smartha Brahman)
Solanum nigrum	*gaNike huuvu*[90]	Flower in Oil Presser funeral garland
Tamarindus indicus [tamarind]	*huNise*	Used to remove ritual pollution(*)

---

[90] Alternate spelling: *gaaNike huuvu* (Helen Ullrich, personal communication)

FEEDING COOKED RICE TO THE ANCESTORS

In Karnataka, as elsewhere, Hindu families of all castes make annual offerings to ancestors. Ancestor ceremonies are done for elders of all preceding generations. Brahmans usually do these ceremonies on the death anniversaries of their most recently deceased parents. Non-Brahmans and A.K.s do special ceremonies at the first anniversary of a death, and thereafter during annual Pitra Paksha (Maladahabba) festival in the lunar months of Bhadrapada or Asvija (September-October). Popular times for this festival are a few days after the full moon of Bhadrapada, or on the new moon day at the beginning of Asvija.

The deceased elders and others worshipped on this occasion are regarded as spiritual beings who, people hope, are contented and settled in the after-life as benign spirits similar to deities. They are, however, thought to be hungry; and they can become angry if not fed, according to the people we interviewed. They also need new clothes every year, we were told, so they can make a dignified appearance when meeting with deities.

A detailed account of ancestral ceremonies can be found in my book, *Coloured Rice* (Hanchett 2023). The ancestors, both male and female, receive food (*(y)eDe*), and other offerings in two different ways. Among non-Brahmans and the Scheduled Caste, they are represented by one or two *kaLashas* – small vessels filled with water and topped with betel leaves and a whole coconut. One vessel, or the only one if only one is set out, is called a 'married woman vessel' (*muTTayide kaLasha*), and it may have a *taaLi* on it. It is also draped with a garland of flowers, usually **yellow chrysathemums**. The vessel is set onto a platform (*hase maNe*) which has been sprinkled with **raw rice**. Special designs (*rangoli*) are drawn on the floor underneath it.

Among Brahmans, the ancestors are represented by actual human beings, other Brahmans, who have done a 24-hour water and food fast. They eat food at the home of the family performing the ceremony after being ritually transformed into the ancestor being propitiated.

The meals offered are as elaborate as possible, with multiple vegetable preparations, sweets, and so on. Multiple meals – three or more -- are offered in non-Brahman and Scheduled Caste ceremonies. One of these meals is eaten by an animal – a crow on the roof usually, or the family cow (in one home we interviewed) – <u>before</u> the family themselves eat.

The most prominent plant items in these ceremonies are **cooked and raw rice, cucumber, chrysanthemums,** broken **coconuts,** and the tip (*suli*) of a **plantain leaf,** on which food is served. Cooked rice is the one item found in the offered meals of all castes. The ritual setting in non-Brahman and Scheduled Caste homes has a row of longitudinally sliced cucumbers set behind it, as shown in Figure 37.

Specific vegetables (cooked in the stir-fry preparation called *palya*) are either required or tabooed for this feast. While each caste has its own requirements and taboos, and some taboo those required by others, all seem to have some such rules. The most frequently required vegetables in our sample of 15 households were **bottle gourd** (*sorekaayi*), *Momordica charantia* (Kannada *hagalakaayi*), **brinjal/eggplant,** and **potato. Unripe plantain** (*baaLekaayi*) was required in three households. (Hanchett 2023, Table 32) One Weaver caste family requires **whole Bengal gram** (*kaDale kaaLu*) to be mixed with the unripe plantain in their ancestral *palya* preparation.

The most frequently tabooed (by three to five households) vegetables for ancestor feasts were *Luffa acutangula* (Kannada *hirekaayi*), the **common gourd** (*kumbalakaayi*), **dried bottle gourd** (*halsorekaayi*), and **okra (*bendekaayi*)**. Some families also considered the pumpkin (*kumbalakaayi*) to be unsuitable for ancestors' meals.

<u>Discussion</u>. While ancestor worship is not a rite of passage, properly speaking, it does represent people's vision and hope for a satisfactory culmination of a human life, and its evolution into a benign spirit who will help rather than harm the living. The items included as offerings are familiar from other rituals.

The cultural logic, if any, of using (or not using) specific vegetables is neither conscious nor obvious. Most people will say these are just customs, or that the ancestors are somehow known to like or dislike some foods. Nonetheless, certain patterns are noteworthy. One is the importance of the botanical family Cucurbitaceae in this group of rituals: growth of vines is easily comparable to associated with purity and tranquility. The forbidden *Luffa acutangula* has seeds that are white when young and black as the vegetable matures, possibly suggesting an inauspicious transition. The basic requirement of all castes that the ancestors be fed plain cooked rice is quite important, of course. Rice is the essence of 'food'. In the Kannada language, the word 'meal' (*uuTa*) implies consumption of rice for most castes, and 'fasting' often means not consuming rice.

Figure 37. Farmer House Ancestor
Offering, Bandipur 1966

Figure 38. 'Married
Woman' *kaLasha*
(drawing by Carol
Francis, from a
photograph)

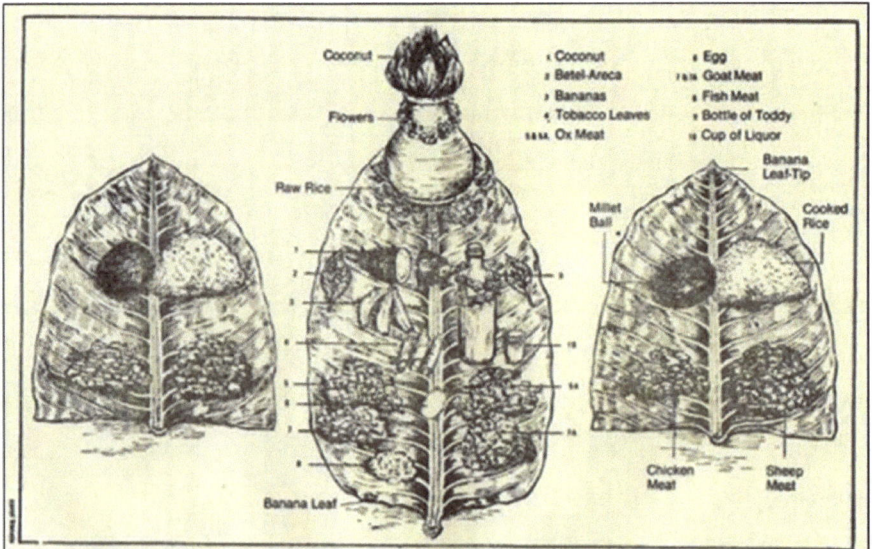

Figure 39. Ancestor Meals Offered in a Scheduled Caste Home
(from a drawing by H. Bettaiah, Bandipur 1967)

Figure 40. Bitter Gourd (*Momordica charantia*), a Common Requirement

Figure 41. *Luffa acutangula*: <u>Not</u> Served to Ancestors (Photo Source: By Nayan j Nath - Own work, CC BY-SA 4.0, https://commons.wikim edia.org/w/index .php?c urid=122715168)

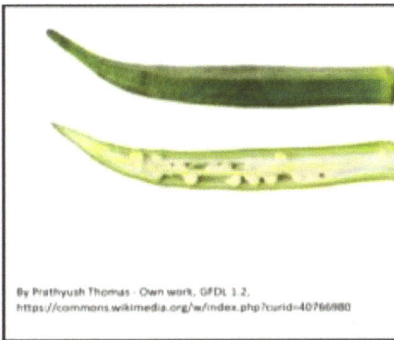

Figure 42. *Hibiscus esculentis*: Not Served to Ancestors

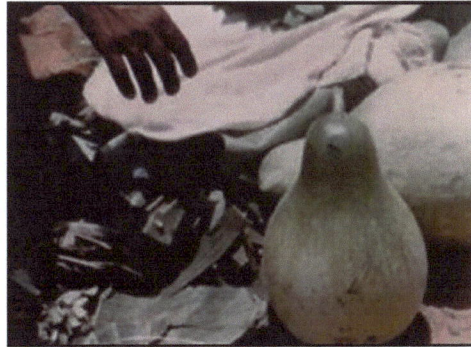

Figure 43. Bottle Gourd (*Lagenaria siseraria*), a Common Requirement for Ancestor Meals

The basic requirement of all castes that the ancestors be fed plain cooked rice is quite important, of course. Rice is the essence of 'food'. In the Kannada language, the word 'meal' (*uuTa*) implies consumption of rice for most castes, and 'fasting' often means not consuming rice.

Table 8. Plant Materials Used in Ancestor Ceremonies

Botanical Name & English	Kannada Name	Uses
Chrysanthemum indicum Chrysanthemum	*šaavantige huuvu* - flower	Strung as a garland over or around the vessel (*kaLasha*) representing the ancestors (yellow color preferred).
Cicer aretinum Bengal gram	*kaDale kaaLu* - whole gram	A required ingredient in vegetable preparation offered to ancestors (one house)
Cocos nucifera Coconut	*tengin kaayi* - fresh coconut	-A broken coconut is set on each leaf-meal offered to ancestors.
Cucumis sativus Cucumber	*sautekaayi*	-Longitudinal slices set behind the ancestral shrine that receives worship and food offerings.
Lagenaria siseraria Bottle gourd	*sorekaayi*	Frequently required among cooked foods offered to ancestors
Momordica charantia Bitter gourd	*hagalakaayi*	Frequently required among cooked foods offered to ancestors

Table 8. Plant Materials Used in Ancestor Ceremonies

Botanical Name & English	Kannada Name	Uses
Musa sapientum Plantain	*baaLe(y)ele - leaf (suli -* tip of leaf) *baaLekaayi* - unripe plantain	-Cooked foods are set on plantain leaves as offerings to ancestors. -Required as an ingredient in cooked foods offered (three out of 15 houses)
Oryza sativa Rice	*akki - raw rice anna -* cooked rice	-The *kaLasha* vessel sits on a bed of raw rice. -Cooked rice is a firm requirement for ancestor meals in all castes.
Solanum tuberosum Potato	*aalugeDDe*	Frequently required among cooked foods offered to ancestors
Solanum melongena Brinjal/Eggplant	*badanekaayi*	Frequently required among cooked foods offered to ancestors

Table 9. Plant Materials Forbidden in Many Ancestor Ceremonies

Botanical Name & English	Kannada Name
Abelmoschus esculentus *Okra*/Lady's finger	*bendekaayi*
Cucurbita spp. Pumpkin	*kumbalakaayi*
Lagenaria siseraria Bottle gourd	*haalsorekaayi* - dried-up bottle gourd
Luffa acutangula Sponge gourd, Rag gourd	*hirekaayi*

APPEASING DANGEROUS SPIRITS

In *Coloured Rice*, I discussed some annual rituals intended to appease deities, all female ones, who are believed to be easily angered. Their destructive power became evident to me when I saw a small **banana tree** used to absorb the dangerous look of the goddess Maramma:

> The *amma* shoots and kills from her eyes. It is through her glance that her destructive anger is most able to turn all to blood and waste. I first realised this while observing a procession for Mari in Chinnapura. As a gaggle of marching villagers returned from the river, where the goddess had been bathed, it stopped in the middle of a dusty hill. Someone had placed a small banana tree, cut from its base, in the path before them. Everyone waited. What were they waiting for? I asked. They explained in hushed tones that the tree, instead of they themselves, was now getting the angry stare of the goddess. (Hanchett 2023:188)

Some of these goddesses are believed to threaten the well-being of certain families. Therefore, ceremonies for them, unlike rites of passage or ancestor worship, were done only by some, not all, households. Those we observed were all done for goddesses known, like Maramma, to be easily angered or for ghosts of females who had been murdered or died in some other unnatural way. Mastiamma, for example, was generally thought to be the restless spirit of a pregnant woman accidentally killed by a hunter. The families who performed the rites had been advised to do so by local soothsayers (*mantravadi*), consulted at times of difficulty. Some families conducted their rituals on an emergency basis. Others got into regular relationships with the deities or spirits and performed regularly scheduled (annual or other) rituals to ensure the well-being of their families. One woman, for example, told me why she does this ritual for the goddess Piriyapattanadamma:

> The bad feelings of Piryapattanadamma have a striking effect on Mrs. S.'s home. Before they started up the ritual again, too many cattle were dying. [16] She summed up the problem in a highly symbolic (and familiar) image: "If we do not worship this goddess, our cows' milk won't come. Only blood comes." (Hanchett 2023:205)

Some families conducted their ceremonies on the pattern of ancestor worship. In one case, the spirit, Mastiamma, being propitiated was thought to be an ancestor reborn as the goddess; and 12 Farmer families of the same patrilineage joined annually to propitiate her. They shared their story with me:

> In our *vamsa* [largest possible patrilineal group] there was once a woman named Chennajjamma. She was the eldest daughter-in-law. She was pregnant. Her husband did something wrong, and was taken to court. She became frightened about him and panicked. Before they could settle the case, she jumped into the village tank and drowned.

> When she was jumping, a man named Iranna, a servant *(pyun)*, had been watching. He jumped into the tank in hopes of saving her life. But he failed and was also drowned.

Later on Chennajjamma was reborn as a goddess on the same spot where she had jumped into the tank. And Iranna became a god. There is a Mastiamma stone at that spot.

We have to make offerings to that stone on special occasions. So when we want to make a marriage, we set all the clothing and jewels there. You see, she was a daughter-in-law of our house.

Or if a calf is born into the house, we give the first milk there, pouring it over the stone. If we don't do that, the cow will produce blood instead of milk. (Hanchett 2023:218-219)

Offerings to these spirits take various forms. Some are done on the mode of ancestral rites. For example, one Farmer caste man we met had murdered a Scheduled Caste woman in the past. When trouble came to his family, he decided to conduct an ancestor ceremony for her in the manner done by the Scheduled Caste, which involved eating some beef. Another ancestral-style ritual is done for Mastiamma by the Farmer caste family. Other families may just offer food and *puja* worship. It is important that all of these rituals are performed outdoors, not in houses.

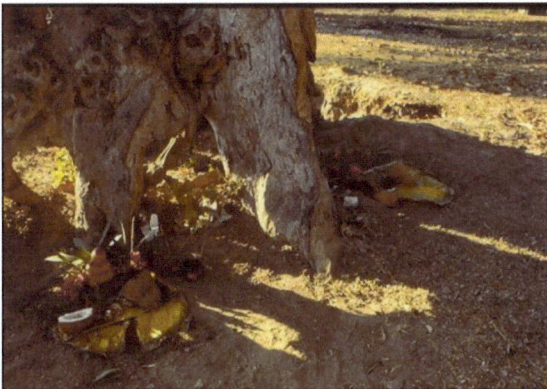

Figure 44. Outdoor Meal Offered to Goddess Piriyapattanadamma

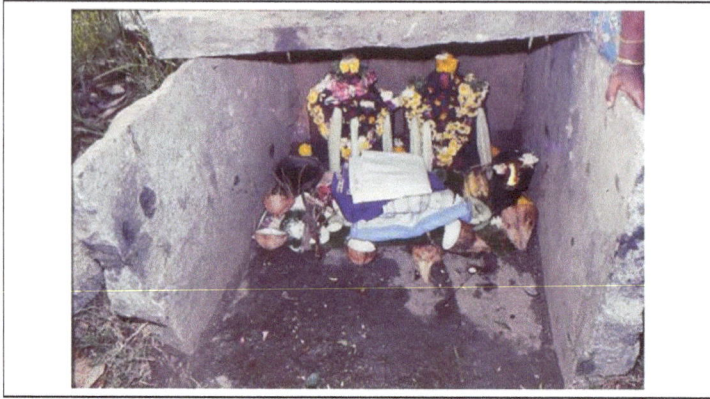

Figure 45. Ancestral-type Offering to Goddess
Mastiamma at an Outdoor Shrine

Plumeria Flower. Photo by Bchachara - Own work, CC BY-SA 4.0,
https://commons.wikimedia.org/w/index.php?curid=114673181

Figure 47. *Plumeria rubra* flower,
Kannada deyya kaNigal huuvu

Figure 46. *Nerium
indicum:* Kannada
kaNigal huuvu

Figure 48. *Calotropis gigantea* flower: Kannada, *(y)ekkadahuuvu*
(https://commons.wikimedia.org/wiki/File:Calotropis_gigantea_in_Be
lur_Math,_Howrah,_West_Bengal.jpg#/media/File:Calotropis_gigante
a_in_Belur_Math,_Howrah,_West_Bengal.jpg)

There are certain flowers required as offerings to these "amma" goddesses.[91] The **oleander** and the **plumeria** are especially important. They are both called by the same name, *kaNigalhuuvu.* The oleander (*Nerium indicum*) is 'red *kaNigal*', and the plumeria is 'white *kaNigal*' or *deyya kaNigal.* Other flowers, fruits, and foods are offered; but the *kaNigal* flower is required.

Figure 49. *Calotropis gigantea* Plant (https://commons.wikimedia.org/wiki/Fil e:Ankhada_Plant_with_full_bloom.jpg#/ media/

Another flower associated with these goddesses is **crown flower**, or **milkweed** (*(y)ekka* in Kannada), *Calotropis gigantea.* The poisonous sap is used as an antiseptic. One man, of the Oil Presser caste, told me in 1976 that, "Inside this tree there is a Mari at all times, so demons (*devvas*) won't come near it. Women should never go near the 'white' *(y)ekka.*" He said that it is only the leaves that are used for worship, not the flower, although others may use the flower. A piece of this plant, or of its root, is used by some people as an amulet to protect

---

[91] A woman of the Oil Presser caste told me in 1976 the the goddesses who require these flowers are Mariyamma (Maramma), Mastiamma, Pleeginamma, Byaedaramma, Sookinamma, MiDichilamma, "etcetera – all the *ammas.*"

cattle, so that 'bad winds' (*sonku*) from demons will not come to them.[92]

Another man, a Saivite of the Weaver caste, had a more positive opinion about this plant. He told me that the 'white' *(y)ekka* is a 'holy' plant, because the carpels and stamens (*kusume*) are in the shape of a linga. In Bengaluru I met a woman selling the flowers in a market. She said they were definitely <u>not</u> to be used in the hair, just for worship. A woman standing nearby said the flower was special for the god Ganesha. I was told that there were both 'red' and 'white' types of *(y)ekka*, but I do not have photos of the two different types. (The color of the *(y)ekka* flower in Figure 48 is considered to be 'a little red and a little white', according to one informant.)

A priest at the Bandipur Maramma temple told me in 1976 that this goddess very much likes the leaves of the **neem** tree (*Azadirachta indica,* or *beevu* in Kannada). The reason for this, he explained, is the structure of the plant, the three-leaf type known as *patre*. If the goddess possesses someone, he continued, that person must eat some of this leaf, as it is 'cooling'. Any type of flower, including the oleander or plumeria is suitable for offerings to this goddess, except for one: *Thevetia peruviana* (*balasampige* in Kannada) is <u>not</u> a suitable offering.

---

[92] The term *sonku* can also refer to an infection or contagious disease, especially an infection spread by air. (Helen Ullrich, personal communication)

Table 10. Plant Materials Associated with Restless *Amma* Spirits

Botanical Name	Kannada Name	Required/Forbidden
Azidrachta indica Neem	*beevin(y)ele* - leaf	Required by Maramma because of its three-leaf form, according to a priest in her temple.
Calotropis gigantea Crown flower, Milkweed	*(y)ekkadahuuvu* - flower	Often used in worship for these goddesses; not used for women's ornamentation.
Cucumis sativus Cucumber	*sautekaayi*	Required if the ceremony is done in the style of ancestor propitiation
Nerium indicum Oleander	*kaNigal huuvu* - flower	Firm requirement for all offerings to this group of deities; not used for women's ornamentation.
Plumeria rubra Plumeria, Frangipani	*deyya kaNigal huuvu* - flower	Firm requirement for all offerings to this group of deities; not used for women's ornamentation
Thevetia peruviana	*balasampige*	Not acceptable as an offering to Maramma, according to the priest in her temple.

Part II

REVIEW AND SUMMARY

The Most Commonly Used Plants in Family Rituals

As living beings, plants greatly help in rites of passage and other rituals intended to perpetuate and protect a family line. They may serve to bless those going through a transition, as in the case of rubbing turmeric powder and oil on a bride's face. They can serve as stand-ins for humans, shattered to remove danger from the 'evil eye' (*drišti*), a job generally done by ripe coconuts. They may confirm or legitimize a transition. They may be used to express a strong commitment to tradition, as in the marriage of a Daas initiate to a sacred fig tree. Tying a piece of turmeric or a betel leaf onto the wrist of a bride or bridegroom expresses commitment to their marriage and the many social relationships affected by it. A plantain leaf is universally considered to be the only suitable place for food offered to deities and other spirits, such as ancestors. A bed of raw rice underneath a wooden platform (*hase maNe*) clearly signifies the importance of the ritual for the person seated there.

In this group of required plant species, there are some that function one way or another in all of the rites of passage described above: coconut, plantain, turmeric, areca, betel leaf, Bengal gram, and rice. A common expression, *haNNu-kaayi*, meaning 'fruit and coconut', is used as a kind of shorthand way of describing all sorts of ritual offerings. These seven plants appear in different forms, and different plant parts may be used in different ways in different rituals.

Coconut (*Cocos nucifera*)

The coconut seems to be the most used: its fruit at various stages of development (tender, with the outer husk/endocarp; ripe; or dried) and its flower. It also is an ingredient in some ritually required foods, such as the *kaDale husli* preparation distributed during the Iyengar Brahman cradle ritual. Coconuts in various stages of development are used in the 'lap filling' rituals that celebrate the maturation of a young girl, the imminent marriage for a bride, and the impending birth for a woman in the seventh month of her first or second pregnancy. A bridegroom brings ripe coconuts to the meeting at which his wedding date is set. One or two ripe coconuts are held in the joined hands of a bride and groom as guests congratulate them and express their good wishes by pouring a milk-ghee mixture over the fruit(s). Coconut flowers, in this region are used only in death rituals. They can be seen in the *tithi* ritual as performed 11 days after a death by almost all castes, as far as we could determine.

The draining out of a ripe coconut's 'water' in some funerary rites vividly represents the loss of a human life.[93] In ancestor ceremonies of non-Brahman and Scheduled Caste families, the ancestors are represented by one or two small *kaLashas* – pots of water that are topped with some betel leaves and a coconut. And broken coconuts are always set onto the meals offered to them. The coconut thus serves

---

[93] In this study area, Oil Pressers do this at the grave, and Smartha Brahmans, at the cremation place.

to represent a human life, both the good and the bad possibilities, hopefully absorbing some of the bad, so that humans can survive and thrive.[94]

Figure 50. Five *kaT* (tied packets) of Betel Leaves, on a Plate with Plantains (upper left). Weaver caste wedding, Bandipur 1967 (photo by Doranne Jacobson, International Images)

Figure 51. Botanical Drawing of Coconut Tree, and Fruit with and without the endocarp

Figure 52. Powdered Turmeric, Sold at the Weekly Village Market, Bandipur 1976

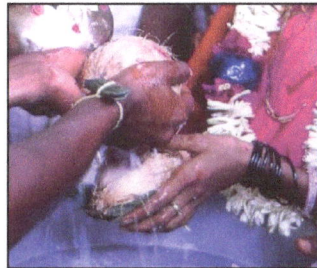

Figure 53. Betel Leaf *kankaNa* on Bridegroom's Wrist, Bandipur 1967 (photo by Doranne Jacobson, International Images)

---

[94] Shakti M. Gupta (2010) argues that destroying coconut fruits became an important part of ritual practice as people of South Asia abandoned human sacrifice.

147

Plantain (*Musa sapientum*)

Plantain fruits, ripe or green, and plantain leaves also function in one way or another in all the rites of passage for which we have information. After a baby of the Farmer caste has been moved out of its first winnowing fan bed into a cradle, the actual place where it was born is honored with offerings that include five bunches of ripe plantains, betel leaves, and areca nuts. Ripe plantains also are distributed to guests. In an Iyengar Brahman house, a plantain leaf is set under the baby's new cradle and covered with raw rice, five sets of betel and areca, and some salted Bengal gram. Ripe plantains are among the items presented to a newly matured girl, a bride, or a pregnant woman in the 'lap-filling' ritual. A bridegroom's family brings ripe plantains to the meeting at which the wedding date is set. In non-Brahman burials, a deceased person's face and torso are generally covered with plantain leaves before the grave is filled in. At least one non- Brahman caste, the Smiths, customarily requires a preparation made with green plantains for funeral feasts. In ancestor ceremonies, cooked foods are offered on the tips (*suli*) of plantain leaves. Foods offered to ancestors often include preparations made with green plantains. Ripe plantains, it seems, are not part of ancestor rituals. Nor do they appear in offerings to dangerous goddesses who threaten family well-being.

Turmeric (*Curcuma longa*)

Turmeric application clearly signifies "auspiciousness," a state of profound importance in this culture. Married women who participate in rites of passage are regularly presented with turmeric powder and vermilion on ritual occasions. Turmeric-colored clothing is worn by

Brahman and Smith caste boys during their sacred thread ceremonies, strongly demonstrating their positive value to society at this auspicious time. In an Iyengar Brahman ceremony associated with a boy's sacred thread ceremony, some married women pound turmeric rhizomes into powder. Turmeric is important in seventh month pregnancy rituals. And every being, human or deity, is sprinkled with turmeric-colored rice (*akšate*) several times during auspicious rituals. A husband and wife, for example, are sprinkled with this mixture during the pregnancy ritual. In marriage rites turmeric is very important, of course. Brides or grooms are smeared with mixtures of turmeric and oil in preliminary rituals, for example. A turmeric root, as mentioned above, signifies commitment when tied to the wrist of a bride, a bridegroom, or a Daas boy initiate as a *kankaNa*. This same rhizome, used to write a name in a bed of rice, confirms the personhood of a newly born infant. We saw a whole turmeric rhizome tied to ritual pounding sticks in a ceremony for the *airaNe* water pots brought to witness and bless the wedding in a Shepherd caste wedding. Turmeric is not a standard part of funerals, except in the case of a widow being rubbed with it before her husband's burial. It is removed from her face at the grave, where she becomes a widow. We did not find any turmeric used in ancestor ceremonies or in rituals for restless goddesses. Nor is it evident in girls' maturation ceremonies, perhaps because of its strong association with the married woman status.

Betel leaves (*Piper betle*)

Betel leaf paired with areca nut is a popular and refreshing combination often eaten after meals. We found it among the offerings in all of the rites of passage we studied, except for boys' maturation rituals (it may be used there too, but our notes do not mention it). The reasons for such betel-areca offerings are clear. Spirits and humans alike are assumed to enjoy chewing this, especially with some tasty spices or other additions. The combination is offered even to cradles in some castes' birth and naming rites. A bridegroom brings betel leaves together with areca nuts to the meeting at which his marriage date is set.

However, the betel leaf also appears at times without areca nuts. Packets of betel, tied with strings (*kaT*) are an essential part of the *(y)ecca* food offerings made by affines (in-laws) to the family of a newly matured girl, for example. These same packets are required in the 'lap filling' ritual for a woman in her seventh month of pregnancy ritual, and also for a bride, according to our information. And a betel leaf (instead of a turmeric rhizome) can be tied to the wrists of bride and bridegroom during their wedding as *kankaNa*. (Figure 53) In auspicious rituals, packets (*kaT*) of betel leaves are used in multiple sets, usually with odd numbers – three or five especially. (Figure 50) In funerals, a single betel-areca set is ritually buried on the path to the grave.

After a non-Brahman burial, however, betel-areca is distributed to mourners as a refreshment after they have bathed in the river. Betel-areca is part of the meal offered to ancestors in non-Brahman and Scheduled Caste homes. It surely is given to the Brahmans who eat on behalf of the ancestors in Brahman homes too, but our notes do not mention it. If restless goddesses are provided with ancestral offerings, they too will receive the betel-areca treat.

Areca (*Areca catechu*)

The areca nut, popular as it is, is rarely used in rites of passage, except when offered in combination with betel leaves. The areca flower (*hombaaLe*), however, is prominent in some auspicious celebrations, especially in the Daas boy's initiation and in weddings. We do not have any record of its being used in girls' maturation ceremonies, however. Clusters of areca flowers set into the mouth of a *kaLasha* vessel are prominent in almost all rituals associated with marriage.

Figure 54: Coconut Flowers (Kannada, *hombaaLe*)

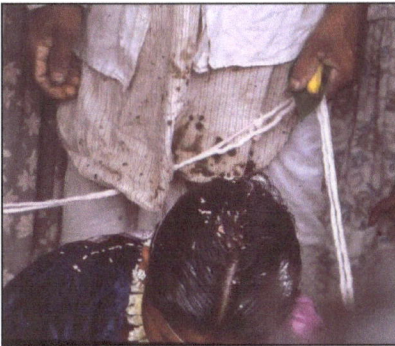

Figure 55. Turmeric-colored Rice (*akshate*) in the Hair of a Scheduled Caste Bride, Bandipur, 1967

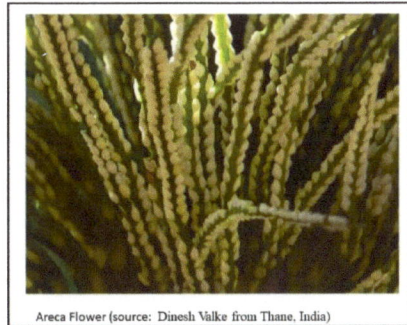

Areca Flower (source: Dinesh Valke from Thane, India)

Figure 56. Areca Flowers (Kannada, *hombaaLe*)

151

Bengal gram (*Cicer arietinum*)

Bengal gram is a common food item. Its importance in almost all rites of passage, however, sets it apart from other types of *Dal* or grams.

Bengal Gram in Auspicious Rituals. We found soaked Bengal gram as an ingredient in a customary snack served after an Iyengar Brahman cradle ritual. In an Iyengar boy's sacred thread ritual, soaked Bengal gram, mixed with jaggery, is set on top of betel leaves at one stage of the proceedings; and in a Smith caste sacred thread ceremony, when Bengal gram flour is distributed to other boys who participate. The gram appears in 'lap-filling' ceremonies for newly matured girls of both Farmer and Scheduled castes, and also for brides of several castes.

Bengal Gram In Inauspicious and Ancestor Ceremonies. In funeral rituals Bengal gram – in its "puffed" form (*kaDale puri*) is sprinkled onto the corpse and on the ground along the path to the grave. Scheduled caste families of the Daas sect require this gram, in its "puffed" form, in an outdoor meal served on the fifth day after a death. We do not have any reference in our notes to this gram being used in ancestor ceremonies; nor is it part of rites to appease difficult or dangerous goddesses. It is noteworthy that the gram is used in its soaked form in auspicious rituals, but in its "puffed" form primarily at funerals.

Rice (*Oryza sativa*)

Rice grains are spread and sprinkled on many surfaces during all rites of passage: especially paddy, raw rice (*akki*), and rice colored with turmeric (*akśate*). Rice is set out on plates and under the wooden platform on which an honored person sits. It is also set under an infant's cradle, when he or she first lies in it.

Rice in Auspicious Rituals

Plain raw rice (*akki*) or rice mixed with turmeric powder (*akshate*) is "put" onto the knees, shoulders, and heads of young people going through auspicious life transitions. A mixture (*accande* or *daanya*) of rice paddy, finger millet, and horse gram is presented to a baby by its maternal uncle or its father in Farmer caste rites; and the same mixture is tied in a cloth bundle to the cradle of a new baby in Scheduled Caste homes. The use of paddy in this context is especially interesting, as it is rice in its "unhusked" state, *i.e.*, before it is ready to be eaten -- just as a baby is a very new, not yet named member of human society. The validating importance of rice is especially evident in the Brahman custom, mentioned above, of writing a baby's name with a turmeric rhizome into a bed of rice. "Puffed" rice (*puri*) is used in Scheduled Caste "lap-filling" rituals for newly menstruating girls. And soaked, sweetened raw rice (*nene akki*) is required as part of the initiation ritual of a boy of the Farmer caste Daas sect. Raw rice is an essential part of the 'lap-filling' rituals done for newly menstruating girls, brides, and women in the seventh month of pregnancy. Ritually pounding of rice paddy is done during one caste's (Farmers of the Sect) marriage rituals – before installation of the *airaNe* water vessels that are an important presence in weddings. A newly married couple of the Barber caste sits beneath a sacred fig tree, putting their hands onto a bed of raw rice before their turmeric-rhizome *kankaNa* bracelets are removed and tied to a branch of the tree.

Rice in Death Ceremonies and Ancestor Worship. Raw rice is set onto the chest of a person's body as he/she is carried to the grave among two of the three castes for which we have detailed information about this. And it is customary for Smartha Brahmans to put some rice into the mouth of a corpse before cremation. These uses are generally parallel to other rites of passage. In ancestor ceremonies, some raw rice underlies the *kaLasha* vessel representing the ancestors, but cooked rice is an essential offering. Cooked rice also can be found in meals associated with other rites of passage, of course, but feeding *is* the ritual for ancestors. Some rituals for dangerous goddesses involve offering an ancestral-style offering; and feeding a special meal (with cooked rice) is part of other family rituals for them as well.

Mango leaves

A string (*toraNa*) of mango leaves always is put above the front door of a home celebrating an auspicious occasion, such as a birth or maturation ceremony. A leafy mango branch is a requirement for the shed under

Figure 57. String of Mango Leaves on a House Door, for an auspicious event (Bandipur, 1967)

which a newly matured non-Brahman girl sits. Another common use of the mango leaf is in pollution removal. Brahman religious specialists often use a mango leaf to sprinkle a newly cleaned house with some kind of liquid (milk and ghee, water, or cow urine) to fully remove birth pollution.

Symbolic Uses of Some Other Plants and Plant Parts

Along with the seven most commonly used plants and plant parts, some others deserve special attention in this review: specific flowers; grains; two grasses; branches and twigs; one whole plant; and three fig trees.

Flowering plants and flowers

Flowers are used to decorate all ritual settings, and married women are expected to wear some types of flowers in their hair. Some well known flowers, such as *tuLasi* (*Ocymum sanctum*) or jasmine are used in various ways here, as elsewhere in India. However, some types of flower usage that are less widely recognized appear in these regional rites.

Garlands

Garlands of flowers are used in both weddings and funerals. In the events that we witnessed, however, there were some differences in colors and type of flowers used. In weddings we observed the garlands to be made of pink and white flowers, but our notes do not indicate which ones were considered most suitable. In one Oil Presser caste funeral that we observed, the corpse's garland was made of *tuLasi*, *Solanum nigrum* (Kannada, *gaaNike huuvu*), and a variety of jasmine (Kannada, *kaakaDa huuvu*). Strands of yellow chrysanthemums were spread on top of the grave; and these same flowers are used in ancestor ceremonies. Because our original observations were made before I pursued the ethnobotany aspect, our notes do not specify further which types of flowers were required or preferred.[95]

Some more obscure plants and their flowers which we found to be customarily used are *Cassia fistula* (Kannada, *kakke*), *Calotropis gigantea* (Kannada, *ekka*), *Leucas indica* (Kannada, *tumbe*), and three flowers named *kaNigal* in Kannada – *Nerium indicum, Plumeria rubra,* and a species of *Salvia* (Kannada, *kashikaNigale*).

Cassia fistula and Calotropis gigantea

One Farmer caste woman, a member of the Mull sect, told us that leaves of both *Cassia fistula* and *Calotropis gigantea* are set (along with a broken coconut and a castor oil lamp) as "offerings" on the place where a birth has occurred. They do this offering on the day when a baby is named and also put into its cradle for the first time. The broken coconut suggests that one purpose of this offering is to avert the 'evil eye' or other spiritual dangers. These two plants appear again in some boys' initiation rites. For example, a Smith caste sacred thread ritual requires *Calotropis gigantea* as one of 'nine sticks' used in a fire ceremony (*homa*). The sticks are dipped into clarified butter and put into the fire by the boy and his parents. The leaves of *Cassia fistula* are required in Daas sect initiations among the Barber and Washerman castes. And the flower of this same plant is used in the Farmer caste rite.[96] We did not find either *Cassia fistula* or *Calotropis gigantea* required in rituals for newly matured girls, however. Nor do they

---

[95] One woman of the Oil Presser caste told me in 1976 that in former times funeral garlands were made of *Hibiscus* flowers, but that this custom is now "disregarded."

[96] All three are using the plant at the riverside ceremonies during which the boy's status as *Daasayya* is confirmed.

appear in our notes on marriage, pregnancy, or ancestor rituals. However, the flower of *Calotropis gigantea* is widely used, along with plumeria and oleander (*Plumeria rubra* and *Nerium indicum,* respectively), as an offering to the difficult and irritable goddesses referred to as *"ammas."* A flower-seller in Bengaluru told me in 1976 that the flower of *Calotropis gigantea* is used only for worship (*puja*), never for "the head" (as women's hair decoration). According to a man serving as priest in 1976 in a Maramma temple in Bandipur, this goddess does <u>not</u> accept the *Thevetia peruviana* (Kannada, *balasampige*) flower.[97] It is interesting that three of the of these four flowers – both those offered and the one tabooed -- are members of the often poisonous "dogbane" (Apocynaceae) plant family.

A man in Bandipur told me that the *Calotropis gigantea* flower is good both for exorcism and for harming one's enemies. The sap is used as an antiseptic, he said, and a 'white' flower of this species is put onto bullocks so that 'bad winds (*sonku*)' will not come from demons (*devvas*). Shakti M. Gupta (2010b:116-117) has found this plant to be associated with women holding swords, and also with the goddess Parvati, in temple iconography. A legend in the *Siva Purana*, she notes, "mentions that Parvati when being pursued by demons, managed to escape by taking refuge in a flower of Arka *i.e.* Calotropis. The Saivites consider this plant very sacred."

Leucas indica

The *Leucas indica* flower is used in some non-Brahman marriage rituals: a Shepherd caste ceremony at the time when *airaNe* water

---

[97] Botanical identification provided by Cecil J. Saldanha.

vessels are being filled; a Farmer caste riverside rite after the marriage has occurred; and a Barber caste ceremony under a sacred fig tree.

In many non-Brahman funerals a whole *Leucas indica* plant (Kannada, *tumbe giDa*) is set onto the head of a grave; and/or it is planted on the path to the grave-site. In an Oil Presser caste funeral, we saw the *Leucas indica* plant set on the grave next to a twig from the *tuLasi* plant (*Ocymum sanctum*). We were told, as mentioned above, that setting this plant on the path to the grave would ensure that "the ghost cannot cross the spot where this stop was made; [it] cannot come back to the village."

Vegetables

Cooked foods are at least as important as the mostly uncooked plant items covered in this study. All rites of passage involve feasting family and community members at some point, and there are some customary foods served on these occasions. This analysis to this point has included little information on very few cooked foods, but Regelson's book, *Food, Community, and the Spirit World* (2022) fills in the gap to some extent.

As discussed above, most castes observe strict requirements and prohibitions for cooked vegetables in the meal offered to ancestors. Two types of gourd, brinjal/eggplant, potato, unripe plantain, and Bengal gram are among the food items frequently required. (See Table 8) Three species are frequently forbidden in the ancestor meal: sponge gourd (*Luffa acutangula*), pumpkin (*Curcubita* spp.), and okra/lady's finger (*Abelmoschus esculentus*). (See Table 9) The bottle gourd (*Lagenaria siseraria*), though required in its fresh form, is prohibited when old and dry. One possible explanation for some of these choices may be color. most of the required vegetables are white. But the pumpkin is red, and this is considered a generally inauspicious color in this part of India.[98] In the case of the bottle gourd, a key may be in its Kannada name (*haalsorekaayi*), which means 'old, worn out bottle gourd'. While the person may grow old and die, the ideal state of the ancestors is serene and actively helpful to their families. The frequent requirement of a preparation (*palya*) made with green, unripe plantains may be significant as well, though possible meanings are elusive. It is interesting to note that the ripe plantains are missing from the ancestors' food offering, though bunches of ripe plantains are found in all auspicious ceremonies for living people.

The raw, fresh cucumber (*Cucumis sativis*), however, is part of the ritual setting for the ancestral offering, and not part of the offered meal(s), though it is widely cooked and eaten on other occasions. A row of cucumbers – cut longitudinally to form long, sharp shapes – lines up beside the ancestral water vessel(s)/*kaLasha* in all non-Brahman and Scheduled Caste ancestor offerings, as far as we know.

Seed Grains, Grams, Pulses, and Buds

We found mixtures of seeds in some castes' birth and marriage rituals. It is common practice among non-Brahmans and Scheduled Caste families to use a mixture (*accande* or *daanya*) of finger millet (*Eleusine coracana*), rice paddy, and horse gram (*Macrotyloma uniflorum*) in the cradle ritual for a new baby. Scheduled Caste families also use 'five kinds of *daanya*', as they call it, in a riverside ritual conducted 30 days after a girl's first menstruation: sorghum (*Sorghum*

---

[98] Widows traditionally wore red saris at the time of this research, though this custom was in decline. Brides wore green and other colors, but never red.

bicolor), finger millet, rice paddy, sesame seeds, and a type of bean. In some castes' marriage rituals, the bride and groom put cumin seeds (*Cuminum cyminum*) on each other's heads, mixed with either sesame seeds (Barber caste) or jaggery (Smartha Brahman). A little game between the bride and bridegroom of the Smith caste involves competingto fish a gold ring out of a pot filled with 'five kinds of grain' (raw rice, *tur Dal*, finger millet, green gram, and areca nut.

According to a Farmer of the Mull sect, germination of three grains – rice paddy, finger millet, and green gram -- is customarily set into the cow dung platform on which the special water pots (*airaNe*) are set as witnesses to a marriage. This caste and some others pound rice paddy as part of this same rite. Pounding and grinding semolina (*rave*) grains, made from wheat, was part of an Iyengar wedding we observed. Bengal gram (*Cicer arietinum*), already discussed above, may be important in rituals because it is a seed. Use of seeds and germination seems especially poetic when marking the occasion of a birth (a new life) or a marriage (a newly formed family unit).

Sesame seeds (*Sesamum indicum*, Kannada *puTTeLLu*) are an ingredient in the *tamTa* smack carried by a new mother of the Farmer caste when she returns with her baby to her husband's house. These seeds also are important in funerals. Sesame seeds may be set onto a plate for a newly deceased family member (Mull Okkaliga custom). They are an ingredient of *pinDa* balls (for Smartha Brahmans), and they may used in the 11th day ritual (Fisherman caste). (See Table 7)

Iyengar Brahmans make use of three different species of fig leaf buds in their seventh month pregnancy ritual. Liquid from a crushed mixture of *Ficus indica, Ficus religiosa, and Ficus glomerata* leaf buds is put into the nostrils of the pregnant woman, on the assumption that this mixture will reach her baby directly. Receiving this mix, I was told, the infant/fetus would "know it was to be born into a Brahman house." Considering the long history and spiritual importance of fig trees in this culture, this interesting custom is one way of connecting future generations to cultural traditions.

Two Grasses

According to one knowledgeable Iyengar Brahman informant, *darbhe* grass (*Poa cynosuroides*) is used in both auspicious and inauspicious ceremonies. He said that a two- strand "grass ring" is put onto corpses, but on other (auspicious) occasions a three-strand grass ring is used. He said that, "There are jokes about this grass's multiple uses," perhaps suggesting some kind of hypocrisy on the part of the plant? The other frequently used grass is called *garike* in Kannada. It is *Cynodon dactylon*. It is frequently inserted into a small mound of cow dung, creating an icon representing the god Ganesh, remover of obstacles.

Sticks and Branches

Tree branches and sticks of various types are prominent ritual items in non-Brahman and Scheduled Caste maturation ceremonies for boys and girls. A girl who has started menstruating, for example, spends some time sitting under a 'flower tent' – as one song describes it--made of leafy country fig, jackfruit (*Artocarpus heterophyllus*), and mango (*Mangifera indica*) branches in the 'outside' part of her family home, as friends and relatives gather to celebrate her transition to womanhood.

Specific sticks also are required for the sacred fire (*homa*) rituals, performed by "twice- born" castes at their sacred thread ceremonies for boys, and probably also on other occasions as well. Tree branches are otherwise also important in boys' maturation rituals. A Brahman boy putting on the "sacred thread" for the first time holds a branch of bastard teak (*Butea monosperma*) in his hand as he makes his initiation vows. A Washerman or Barber caste boy of the Daas sect holds a 'cane stick' of bamboo and a leafy branch of *Cassia fistula* in his hand as a priest taps him on the shoulder and scratches his tongue with a stick of neem (*Azadirachta indica*), confirming his priest-like status as *Daasayya*. Four 'cane sticks' are brought along when a Farmer caste boy goes through his Daas initiation ritual, but our notes do not indicate whether he holds one in the way that the other caste initiates do.

Large posts are used to construct the canopies (*chapra*) set before homes in which a marriage is occurring. Although there must be customary woods used for these structures, our notes do not say much about them. The only information we have on this topic is from a Barber caste wedding in Chinnapura, after which a special ritual was done for one such post, from a country fig tree (*Ficus glomerata*). We were told that this post, "planted in the earth" in front of the house, was "the most important part of the *chapra*."

The folklorist J.A. Abbott, who conducted research in northern Karnataka (then, Mysore) and western Maharashtra, described a belief that planting some trees is considered dangerous, "so dangerous," in fact, "that the young cannot plant them. There are trees that are therefore left to old men to plant."[99] Moslems, he continues, leave the

---

[99] Abbott 1974:329

planting of the tamarind and the *sirih* (*Albizzia lebbek*, as he defines it) and of a small species of margosa to the old. And Hindus, he claims, refuse to plant either the custard apple or the sacred fig at all near their homes.[100] Such customs as these relate the strength and integrity of the family or home to trees, and assign special responsibility for it to elders.

The Sacred Fig Tree

A *Ficus religiosa* tree with a platform built around its base is the first thing one sees when entering either Bandipur or Chinnapura. It is not only a striking feature of the landscape; it is also an object of veneration. People's attachment to this tree comes out in several ways, especially during boys' initiation rituals and marriages.

Figure 58. Sacred Fig Tree with Platform at Village Entrance

Immediately after his initiation ritual, a Farmer or Barber boy of the Daas sect marries a sacred fig tree, graphically signifying his commitment to the tradition that it represents and elevating him to a high social status. A Smith caste boy at the end of his sacred thread ceremony goes to the tree to offer respect and worship. Brahman boys, both Iyengar and Smartha, go to the tree accompanied by another boy,

---

[100] Abbott 1974:329-330

one who has already undergone the ceremony. The initiate is carrying the stick of *Butea monosperma* (Kannada, *muttagada-kone*), which he held while making his vows. Once at the tree, he wedges the stick into the bark of the sacred fig tree. this act is not a 'tree marriage', but it certainly suggests some kind of union.

The sacred fig seems to play a role in all castes' marriages in one way or another. A bride and bridegroom of the Scheduled Caste, for example, go immediately to a sacred fig tree after their *taaLi*-tying ceremony. At the tree they receive blessings from married women and from each other. A bride and bridegroom of the Barber caste also go to the tree after they have shared their first meal as a married couple. Their ritual, as described in Part I, includes tying their turmeric-rhizome *kankaNas* onto the tree itself, attaching a *Leucas indica* (Kannada, *tumbe-huuvu*) flower somehow to the tree, and relatives of the bride and groom pouring the milk-ghee mixture at the base of the tree. This ritual, called *tumbehuuvindhaare*, or 'wedding for the *tumbe* flower', concludes with the bride and groom tucking betel-areca sets into each other's clothes and hair, and then tucking a betel- areca set into the bark of the tree trunk. A ritual of the Mull subcaste of Farmers at the sacred fig tree also includes *Leucas indica,* but our notes do not specify how it is used.

These various rites engage the sacred fig tree directly in the initiation or marriage experience, further demonstrating the profound sense of attachment to the traditions, values, and spiritual principles – some spoken, some not -- that the tree represents here, as elsewhere in India.

PART III

DISCUSSION AND CONCLUSIONS

Discussion

As an anthropologist, I tend to search for psychological or cultural meanings in rituals of the sort described above. Family rituals, as acts of social reproduction, presumably convey coded messages and symbolically repesent cultural values. This material is harder to interpret, however, than are verbal materials such as poems, myths, or ancient treatises on trees and other plants. In rites of passage, plant materials are applied to people, held by people. They are sat on by people, they cover people. They are sprinkled on people, buried with people, and so on. Questions of how one plant item or another came to be used in a specific ritual can only be addressed indirectly, by observing patterns or catching the odd comment of a villager. In my view, ritual is a sort of poetry without words, an art form. Deciphering the elusive meanings of it is a challenging exercise. Searching for psychological or cultural messages or meanings in these ritual acts, difficult as it is, is irresistable to anyone familiar with James G. Frazer's concept of "sympathetic magic."

Conversations with ritual specialists, Brahmans and others, surely would produce more explanations of how and why certain plants are used in they ways they are. These men are widely respected, and their suggestions about the proper conduct of rituals often are followed. In the case of Brahman priests, Sanskritic literature, the *Laws of Manu*, and India's myths provide a basis for some practices. Both of the villages in which we lived had relatively large, well-educated Brahman populations who guided some practices, but not all. In any event, ritual specialists themselves, even Brahmans, have oral traditions that have fed into the highly varied oral traditions of Indian castes and tribes over the centuries. In the case of non-Brahmans and Scheduled Caste priests, priests' knowledge about which flowers the difficult *amma* goddesses like or dislike, for example, is more likely to be based on oral traditions related apparently to goddesses such as Kali.

One general assumption in Hindu oral and literary traditions is that certain trees are inhabited by gods, goddesses, or other spirits (benign or dangerous). According to Upadhyaya (1964:15-16), "in course of time, various gods and goddesses came to be associated with trees and plants and subsequently they began to be worshipped." Thus, trees and plants have been "regarded as animate beings" for a long time in South Asia. Shakti M. Gupta points out that beliefs in "tree spirits" can be found "in most religions all over the world, particularly so in the East." (2010b:112) This also was true in parts of Europe, where oak trees were worshipped until the early 20th century.

Uses of specific plant items raise interesting questions. Why, for example, does the ritual specialist supervising a Daas boy's initiation "scratch his tongue" with a stick of neem (*Azadirachta indica*)? Literature compiled by S.K. Jain and Dr. Vartika Jain (2016) helps by showing that this plant is widely assumed to have cleansing properties. Could the Daas initiation rite be a way of purifying the boy's future speech as a *Daasayya* guiding community members? In the Smith caste sacred thread ceremony, described above, a priest also burns a boy's tongue. In this case it is done with a stick that has been dipped in clarified butter and offered to the sacred fire (*homa*). This act was explained as a way of "removing all defilement the boy may have accrued by eating the food of other castes."

Regarding *Butea monosperma* (Kannada, *muttagada*), a branch of which is held by a Brahman boy during his initiation, our notes do not reveal any explanations for its use. However, the ethnobotany literature discusses both medicinal and ritual uses and meanings. Not only was it mentioned in the Vedas, according to Shakti M. Gupta, but also it is associated with ritual efforts to ensure good pregnancy outcomes or to prevent barrenness in some regions. According to Professor Gupta (2001:11-13), the tree is widely considered to be holy, because its three-leaf growth pattern represents the group of three major Hindu Gods: Brahma, Vishnu, and Siva. It is called *plaksha* in Sanskrit, and it is used in many types of religious ceremonies:

> It is a common practice to use the leaves of the tree in ceremonies connected with blessing the calves to ensure their becoming good milkers? Dry twigs of the plant are used in the sacred fire Homa. It's wood is sacrificial and is mentioned in the Vedas. From the wood are made utensils used for sacred purposes. The staff placed in the hands of a Brahman boy at the time of his thread ceremony is made from the Plaksha wood. When a Brahman renounces the worldly life and becomes a sadhu and his hair are being shorn, he is given the Plaksha leaf to eat or else he must eat off Plaksha leaves. (Gupta 2001:12)

167

The choice of three types of tree branches – country fig, mango, and jackfruit -- to shelter a newly matured girl remains somewhat mysterious. As important as these plants are in many regions of South Asia, the question remains: Why use these three and not some others on this occasion? The country fig (*Ficus glomerata*), for example, unlike the sacred fig or banyan, is mostly used for practical purposes rather than religious ones, although Shakti Gupta (2001:38) says that this tree's parts are widely believed to represent Brahma (roots), Vishnu (bark), and Siva (branches). Perhaps unlike its more frequently worshipped cousins, however, the country fig does have numerous medical uses. Its leaves, bark, roots, fruits, and latex all have healing qualities. (Gupta 2001:38)

The mango tree is a general symbol of fertility, according to Shakti M. Gupta (2010b). And it is the subject of much temple iconography more often than the country fig. It appears in ancient myths, such as the *Puranas*:

> The mango tree in *Brahmasaras* is in the shape of Brahma. He who waters it, leads his *pitris*, ancestors, to salvation. (Gupta 2001:42, citing Dikshitar *Purana Index*, vol. I, p. 166)

Jackfruit (*Artocarpus heterophyllus*), the third type of branch required for girls' maturation ceremonies, is similar to the country fig, in having more practical and medical uses than symbolic ones.[101] Its profusion of fruits and seeds within a large case, however, would seem to make it a logical choice for rituals related to fertility or multiplication.

---

[101] Many are referenced in Jain and Jain 2018:42.

In *Coloured Rice* I discussed the relevance of cultural traditions, especially numerology and color symbolism, to some ritual practices. The color yellow is auspicious, and a black item will attract (or divert) bad luck, evil eye, or ominous spiritual forces. Odd numbers, especially three or five, are part of auspicious rituals, for example. In plant symbolism much is made of the number three, and there is a Kannada name for a plant with a three-leaf growth pattern: *patre*.[102]

As widely used as the coconut fruit is in all Hindu rituals, there is very little discussion in the ethnobotany literature of its uses at different stages of development – tender coconuts *vs.* ripe ones. Various uses of its flower, rather than the similar areca flower, have not been much discussed in the literature. It is generally agreed, however, that the resemblance of the ripe coconut to a human head is definitely associated with its ritual uses. Both Upadhyaya (1964) and Shakti Gupta (2001) argue that sacrificing a ripe coconut came to be more widespread as human sacrifice declined. It seems possible, however, that the resemblance to the human head made the fruit a logical ritual choice even if actual human sacrifice had not been practiced.

Similar issues arise with rice (*Oryza sativa*), which is used in numerous different forms in the rites of passage described above.[103] According to Shakti M. Gupta, only "new rice" is used for rituals, not older rice, which is preferred for cooking. (2001:61)[104] She also points

---

[102] According to Helen Ullrich (personal communication), there are some plants called patre in Kannada which do not have a three-leaf growth pattern.

[103] As paddy, raw rice, granulated rice, rice mixed with turmeric, cooked rice, and as rice flour for painting floor designs on some occasions.

[104] Our notes do not indicate whether this is/was true in my study area or not, but it seems to be the general Karnataka preference. (Helen Ullrich, personal communication).

out that rice is a more or less universal fertility symbol in human cultures, and often is associated with wealth. (2001:60) As significant as rice is, and probably always has been, in Hindu rituals, there is not much discussion in the ethnobotany literature to date on use of it in its different stages of development, from paddy to cooked rice, in different types of rituals.

Other plant items, such as Bengal gram (*Cicer arietinum*), do not seem to be as widely used elsewhere in symbolic ways as they are/were in our Karnataka field locations; so there are few hints in the literature about what the many ritual uses of this popular food gram may signify. A similar problem exists in the case of cumin (*Cuminum cyminu*), which has many documented medical uses but no ritual ones, in the available literature. (Jain and Jain 2018:109-110) In the case of funerals, the assumption that *Leucas indica* (Kannada, *tumbe giDa*) can block the return of a potentially dangerous ghost, also seems difficult to explain. In Jain and Jain's *Compendium of Indian Folk Medicine and Ethnobotany*, this plant is shown to have numerous medical uses in all regions of South Asia, and to be used as a ritual offering to Siva and other deities in a few places, including Karnataka.

As in other regions of India, a ritual may include some kind of "marriage" between a human and a tree, or two humans of the same sex. As discussed in the Introduction, at least one anthropologist, Dr. Venkatesan (2021), has managed to elicit comments on this type of practice from a priest, who expressed the view that trees are reborn souls.

Many other gestures of connection with the sacred fig tree are found in marriages and puberty rites we studied in Karnataka. Among some castes, as discussed above, it is customary for the bride and groom to visit a sacred fig tree after their marriage is completed, leaving some of the items signifying commitment – their *kankaNa* bracelets – in the tree. And Brahman boys put their special *Butea monosperma* sticks into the crevices of the tree's bark after the sacred thread ceremony.

Along with mythology and visual imagery, an anthropologist seeks social explanations for ritual practices, or analysis of the social consequences of rituals. For example, Anthony Good (1982) has discussed a Tamilnadu custom of marrying a pre-pubescent girl to another girl. Relating this to other such irregular "marriage" rituals elsewhere, he argues that marrying a girl to another girl (or to a plant or an inanimate object) formally breaks the tie between her and her natal family, making it unnecessary for her to observe death pollution, and making it unnecessary for her family to observe such restrictions when she dies later on in life.[105] This sort of explanation, applied to the Daas boy's marriage to a sacred fig tree, may be helpful. Perhaps the implication is that he is now an adult, dedicated to the traditions that the sacred fig represents, capable of independent action, and ready to lead others in ritual as a *Daasayya*.

In the 21st century one cannot talk about the world of plants without considering climate change. A strong theme in much ethnobotany literature is conservation and protection of biodiversity, which is an increasingly difficult problem in all world regions, including the sites of this research. Hassan District, Karnataka State, is one of the seven districts of the state most threatened by climate

---

[105] This is a social structural pattern, which has little or no relation to people's emotional responses to losses, of course.

change, according to a recent study by the Karnataka State Forestry Department (EMPRI 2021):

> The Karnataka state action plan on climate change said that around 38 per cent of forest area in the state would be hit by climate change by the 2030s. It also noted that forests in the central and northern parts of the Western Ghats would be impacted by climate change....
>
> The study predicted change in vegetation largely in the scrub and open forest areas of seven districts -- Bijapur, Raichur, Koppal, Bellary, Chitradurga, Kodagu and Hassan -- in both short term (2030) and long term (2080s). The study states the forested grids in these seven districts will be impacted by climate change...
>
> "This means that the future climate at such locations would not be suitable for the existing vegetation or forest type and biodiversity. The forest type change may be accompanied by forest dieback (a condition in which a tree or a shrub begins to die from the tip of its leaves or roots due to unfavourable environment) and mortality"... (Thakur 2021)

Despite the popular and official commitment to protect bio-diversity and forest environments throughout India (and the best efforts of ethnobotanists), the Karnataka State plan is not getting the attention it deserves, according to journalists. A recent article in *The Deccan Herald* is titled, "Karnataka's climate plan gathers dust on Centre's shelf." (Kulkarni 2022)

Conclusions

Many efforts to interpret meanings in these ritual practices must be speculative, as people themselves generally are not inclined to explain their customs. Brahmans have better knowledge than others of mythological and theological reasons for some practices; but they too have unexplained customs, which are not entirely different from those of other caste groups. A further challenge in this type of analysis is the huge variety of practices, every caste and subcaste having its own requirements (*shaastras*). On more than one occasion, we found people even of the same community arguing about points of ritual during the proceedings. General patterns can be found; but universal consensus is nonexistent. Customs thus will continue to evolve.

Nonetheless, this study shows that the plant world is fully intertwined with human life in these agrarian communities. This is true both practically and symbolically. Many of the practices described here reveal a strong feeling that plant growth and human growth are analogous.

Whether their meanings are explicitly stated or merely implicit, numerous plants and plant parts are required (*shaastra*) to move a person from birth, through maturation, marriage, and pregnancy, all the way to death and beyond. Some trees and other plants clearly are perceived as spiritual beings who can help with human life transitions. Our research has found almost 60 different species being used, some in multiple ways (as whole plants, leaves, twigs, branches, roots, seeds, flower buds, flowers, or green or ripe fruits). There is no question that further, detailed inquiry would have revealed even more. Those we did find are listed below in the Glossary. (See Annex-4)

This research study was done almost six decades ago, and there surely have been changes of all sorts introduced by new generations. Yet, people do still get born, mature, marry, and die; and those who care about them certainly will mark these transitions with rituals. The changing ways of using plants and plant materials are continuing to be documented in various regions of India. This story has, nonetheless, offered as thorough a picture as possible of how plants were used at one particular place and time in a diverse community with multiple castes and subcastes.

We thank the people of these two Karnataka Villages for their hospitality. Our note-writing and picture-taking were somewhat disruptive to those whose rituals we observed, and we are forever grateful to them for inviting us to join these intimate celebrations. Others spent many hours providing us with detailed descriptions of customs we were not able to observe directly. They are the true authors of this study, and we hope they can benefit somehow from our documenting their efforts to maintain family continuity and prosperity.

REFERENCES AND BIBLIOGRAPHY

Abbott, J.A.
   1974 The Keys of Power; A Study of Indian Ritual and Belief. Secaucus, New Jersey: University Books.

Ananthakrishna Iyer, Rao Bahadur L.K.
   1935 The Mysore Tribes and Castes, Volume I. Mysore: The Mysore University.

Babb, Lawrence A.
   1975 The Divine Hierarchy: Popular Hinduism in Central India. New York and Lodon: Columbia University Press.

Balick, Michael J.
   1996 Transforming Ethnobotany for the New Millennium. Annals of the Missouri Botanical Garden 83:1:58-66.

Balick, Michael, and Paul Alan Cox
   1997 Plants, People, and Culture; The Science of Ethnobotany. New York: Scientific American Library.

Basham, A.L.
   1976 The Practice of Medicine in Ancient and Medieval India. In Asian Medical Systems: A Comparative Study, Charles

Leslie, ed. Berkeley, Los Angeles and London: University of California Press. pp. 18-43.

Beck, Brenda E.F.
1969 Colour and Heat in South Indian Ritual. Man (n.s.) 4:4:553-572.

Berlin, Brent, Dennis E. Breedlove, and Peter H. Raven
1968 Covert Categories and Folk Taxonomies. American Anthropologist 70:290-299. 1973 General Principles of Classification and Nomenclature in Folk Biology. American Anthropologist 75:1:214-242.

Bhattacharya, Narendra Nath
1980 Indian Puberty Rites; Second edition, revised and enlarged. New Delhi: Munshiram Manoharlal Publishers Pvt. Ltd.

Carman, John B., and Frédérique Marglin
1985 Purity and Auspiciousness in Indian Society. Leiden: Brill.

Conklin, Harold C.
1962 Lexicographical Treatment of Folk Taxonomies. International Journal of American Linguistics 28:2, Part IV, pp.119-141.

Crooke, William
1909 Death; Death Rites; Methods of Disposal of the Dead Among the Dravidian and Other Non-Aryan Tribes of India. Anthropos Bd.4, H.2, pp. 457-476.

Dube, S.C.
1953 Token Pre-puberty marriage in Middle India. Man 53:18-19.

Dubois, Abbe J.A.
   1906 Hindu Manners, Customs and Ceremonies. Oxford: Clarendon Press, third edition.

Dymock, W.
   1890 The Flowers of the Hindu Poets. Journal of the Bombay Anthropological Society 2:80-91.

Eichinger Ferro-Luzzi, Gabriella
   1977 Ritual as Language: The Case of South Indian Food Offerings. Current Anthropology 1:3:507-514.

EMPRI/Environmental Management and Policy Research Institute
   2021 Karnataka State Action Plan on Climate Change, Version 2; Draft Report. Bangalore: Department of Forest, Ecology, and Environment, Government of Karnataka. (https://empri.karnataka.gov.in/storage/pdf-files/ccc/ksapcc%20.pdf)

Frazer, James G.
   1922 The Golden Bough; A Study in Magic and Religion. London: Macmillan and Co. Ltd.

Freed, Ruth S., and Stanley A. Freed
   1980 Rites of Passage in Shanti Nagar. New York: The American Museum of Natural History, Anthropological Papers, Vol. 56, Part 3.

   1993 Thosts: Life and Death in North India. New York: The American Museum of Natural History, Anthropological Papers, No. 72.

Ghate,V.S.

1998 Plants in Patra-Pooja. Ethnobotany 10:6-15.

Gold, Ann Grodzins
2002 Children and Trees in North India. Worldviews 6:3:276-299.

Good, Anthony
1982 The Female Bridegroom: Rituals of Puberty and Marriage in South India and Sri Lanka. Social Analysis 11:35-55.

1991 The Female Bridegroom; A Comparative Study of Life-Crisis Rituals in South India and Sri Lanka. Oxford: Clarendon Press.

Gupta, Shakti M.
2001 Plant Myths and Traditions in India (revised and enlarged edition). Munshiram Manoharlal Publishers Pvt. Ltd.

2010a Floral Motifs Based on Legends. In Manual of Ethnobotany, 2nd revised Edition, S.K. Jain, ed. Jodhpur: Scientific Publishers (India). pp. 119-126.

2010b Woman and Tree Motifs. In Manual of Ethno-botany, 2nd revised Edition, S.K. Jain, ed. Jodhpur: Scientific Publishers (India). pp. 112-118.

Hanchett, Suzanne
1972 Festivals and Social Relations in a Mysore Village; Mechanics of Two Processions. Economic and Political Weekly 7:31-33:1517-1522.

1975 Hindu Potlatches: Ceremonial Reciprocity and Prestige in South India. In Competition and Modernization in South

Asia, edited by Helen E. Ullrich. Delhi: Abhinav. pp. 27-59.

1978a Review: Five Books in Symbolic Anthropology. American Anthropologist 80:3:613- 621.

1978b Recent Trends in the Study of Folk Hinduism and India's Folklore. Journal of Indian Folkloristics (Mysore) 1:1:40-54.

2003a Life Cycle Rituals. In South Asian Folklore: An Encyclopedia; Afghanistan/Bangladesh/India/Nepal/Sri Lanka. Margaret A. Mills, Peter Claus, and Sarah Diamond, eds. New York & London: Routledge. pp. 354-358.

2003b Puberty Rituals. In South Asian Folklore: An Encyclopedia; Afghanistan/Bangladesh/India/Nepal/Sri Lanka. Margaret A. Mills, Peter Claus, and Sarah Diamond, eds. New York & London: Routledge. pp. 492-493.

2023 Coloured Rice; Symbolic Structure in Hindu Family Festivals. Pasadena, CA: Development Resources Press, second edition.

Hanchett, Suzanne, and Leslie Casale
1976 The Theory of Transitional Phenomena and Cultural Symbols. Contemporary Psychoanalysis 12:4:496-507 [on widowhood rituals]

Hanchett, Suzanne, Tofazzel Hossain Monju, Kazi Rozana Akhter, and Anwar Islam

2014 Water Culture in South Asia; Bangladesh Perspectives. Pasadena: Development Resources Press.

Hart, George
1975 The Poems of Ancient Tamil. Berkeley: University of California Press.

Iyengar, Masti Venkatesh
1943 Subanna. Bangalore: Printed at the B.B.D. Power Press.

Jacobson, Doranne, and Susan Snow Wadley
1977 Women in India; Two Perspectives. Columbia, MO: South Asia Books.

Jain, S.K.
1964 The Role of a Botanist in Folklore Rsearch. Folklore 5:145-150.

1975 Medicinal Plants. New Delhi: National Book Trust, second edition.

Jain, S.K., ed.
2010 Manual of Ethnobotany, 2nd Revised Edition. Jodhpur: Scientific Publishers (India).

Jain, S.K.
2015 Dictionary of Indian Folk Medicine and Ethnobotany (with new concepts, dimensions and future prospects of ethnobotany); A Reference Manual of Man-Plant Relationships, Ethnic Groups & Ethnobotanists in India (With 433 Illustrations). New Delhi: Deep Publications.

Jain, Vartika, and S.K. Jain

2016 Compendium of Indian Folk Medicine and Ethnobotany (1991-2015). New Delhi: Deep Public-ations.

Jairazbhoy, R.A.
1964/5 Some Aspects of Tree and Pillar Worship. Journal of the Asiatic Society of Bombay (n.s.) 39/40:249-252.

John, Haritha
2017 Deep Rooted Love: Meet the banyan and mango trees who got married after a 100 year 'live-in'. The News Minute. (https://www.thenewsminute.com/article/deep-rooted-love-meet-banyan-and-mango-trees-who-got-married-after-100-year-live-56787)

Kane, Pandurang Vaman
1930-1962 History of Dharmašâstra, 5 vols. Poona: Bhandar-kar Institute Press.

Khare, R.S.
1963 Folk Medicine in a North Indian Village. Human Organization 22:1:36-40.

Khomdram, S.D. et al.
2011 Ethnobotanical Uses of Lamiaceae in Manipur, India. Ethnobotany 23: 64-69.

Kulkarni, Chiranjeevi
2022 Karnataka's Climate Plan Gathers Dust on Centre's Shelf. Deccan herald, 2 March. (https://www.deccan herald.com/state/top-karnataka-stories/karnatakas-climate-plan-gathers-dust-on-centres-shelf-1086811.html)

Kumar, A., and D.K. Yadav
2004 Significance of Sacred Plants in Shraddh Ritual (Pindadan) in Gaya, Bihar. Ethnobotany 16:103-107.

Leslie, Charles, ed.
1976 Asian Medical Systems. Berkeley: University of California Press.

Mandelbaum, David G.
1970 Curing and Religion in South Asia. Journal of the Indian Anthropological Society 5:1/2:171-186.

Mitra, S.C.
1920 On the Worship of the Pipal Tree in North Bihar. Journal of the Bihar and Orissa Research Society. (Bankipor, Patna)

1927-28 Studies in Plant Myths - On an Aetiological Myth About the Night-flowering Jessamine. Quarterly Journal of the Mythic Society (Bangalore) 18:292-293.

1934-35 Studies in Plant-Myths. Quarterly Journal of the Mythic Society (Bangalore) 24:65-67, 179-80, 288-91, 363-67.

Nair, P. Thankappan
1965 Tree Marriage in India. In Tree Symbol Worship in India; A New Survey of a Pattern of Folk-religion, Sankar Sen Gupta, ed. Calcutta: Indian Publications. pp. 141-147.

Nanjundayya, H.V., and Rao Bahadur Ananthakrishna, Iyer
1930 The Mysore Tribes and Castes, Volume III. Mysore: The Mysore University.

Narasimhachar, S.G.

1952 Latin and Kannada Names of Indigenous Medical Plants of Mysore. Mysore State Department of Agriculture, Botanical Series, No. 1.

Obeysekere, Gananath

1969 The Cultural Background of Sinhalese Medicine. Journal of the Indian Anthropological Society 4:1/2:117-139.

1976 The Impact of Ayurvedic Ideas on the Culture and the Individual in Sri Lanka. In Asian Medical Systems, Charles Leslie, ed. Berkeley: University of California Press. pp. 201-226.

Pal, D.C.

1970 Plants Associated with the "Durga Puja" Ceremony in West Bengal. Journal of the Bengal Natural History Society 36:61-68.

Rajith, N.P. et al.

2009 Ethnobotanic Studies on Coconut Palm (Cocos nucifra L.) with Special Reference to South Kerala. Ethno-botany 21:32-40.

Ramanujan, A.K.

1967 The Interior Landscape. Bloomington & London: Indiana University Press.

Regelson, Stanley

2022 Food, Community, and the Spirit World; An Indian Village Study. Pasadena: Development Resources Press.

Saldanha, Cecil J., and Dan H. Nicolson, eds.

1976 Flora of Hassan District, Karnataka, India. New Delhi & New York: Amerind Publishing Co. Pvt. Ltd.

Sen Gupta, Sankar, ed.

1965 Tree Symbol Worship in India. Calcutta: Indian Publications.

Southworth, Franklin

2005 Linguistic Archaeology of South Asia. London: Routledge Courzon. (Chapter 7, 'Palaeobotanical and Etymological Evidence for the Prehistory of South Asian Crop Plants')

Thakur, Aksheev

2021 Climate Change to Impact Vegetation in 7 Karnataka Districts: Study. Indian Express, 9 November. (https://indianexpress.com/article/cities/bangalore/climate-change-impact-vegetation-karnataka-districts-7614372/) Thurston, Edgar (assisted by K. Rangachari)

1909 Castes and Tribes of Southern India. Madras: Government Press, 7 vols.

Upadhyaya, K.D.

1964 Indian Botanical Folklore. Asian Folklore Studies (Tokyo) 23:2:15-34.

Venkatesan, Souhmya

2021 The Wedding of Two Trees: Connections, Equi-valences, and Subjunctivity in a Tamil Ritual. Journal of the Royal Anthropological Institute (N.S.) 27:478-495.

Yalman, Nur

1964 The Structure of Sinhalese Healing Rituals. In Religion in South Asia, Edward B. Harper, ed. Seattle: University of Washington Press. pp. 115-150.

Zimmer, Heinrich R.
1948 Hindu Medicine. Baltimore: Johns Hopkins Press.

Zimmerman, Francis
1978 From Classic Texts to Learned Practice: Methodological Remarks on the Study of Indian Medicine. Social Science and Medicine 12:97-103 (Discussion by Allen Young, pp. 105-106).

PLANTS AND PEOPLE: KARNATAKA RITES OF PASSAGE

ANNEX -1

CASTE AND SUBCASTE NAMES

English Name	Kannada Name
Brahmans	
Iyengar	(same)
Smartha	(same)
Non-Brahmans	
Barber	Hajamru
Farmer	Jogi Okkaliga
	Mull Okkaliga[106]
	Daas Okkaliga
	Okkaliga
Fisherman	Bestaru
Oil Presser	Ganiga
Shepherd	Kuruba
Smith	Achari
Washerman	Agasaru
Weaver	Devanga
Scheduled Caste	A.K. (Adikarnataka), Holeya
	Daas

---

[106] Mull and Daas are names of religious sects including multiple castes. Mull Okkaligas are devotees of the God Siva, and they strictly avoid drinking alcohol. (Nanjundayya and Ananthakrishna Iyer 1930) Daas sect members are devoted to the God Vishnu.

ANNEX-2

INTERVIEW WITH AN
AYNORU PRIEST

In December 1966, Stanley Regelson interviewed the Aynoru priest who officiated at the Fisherman caste funeral described in Part I. He lived in a neighboring village. He said that his caste was "Vaishnava" or "Sri Vaishnava." The only son of his parents (he had two sisters), he went through a sacred thread (*munji*) ceremony, including having his head shaved and doing a ceremony "like a marriage." From the age of 12 he had worked as a ritual specialist (*pujaari*). He was devoted to the God Anjanayya. He ate meat and offered chickens to Anjanayya. He only knew the Kannada language. He was a bachelor, but could marry. For rituals such as this he was paid in food and money (*dakshiNe*). These ceremonies, he said, must be done by his own hand. If anyone else does them, they will not be "holy." One woman of the bereaved family commented, "We believe only him."

ANNEX-3

BECOMING A BRAHMAN WIDOW: THEN AND NOW

1976 Explanation by an Iyengar Woman

For the first 10 days after her husband dies, a woman does not do anything special. She does not go to the cremation ground. She can use her arasiNa & kum-kum, betel and areca, flowers, *mangalya*, etc.

Married women (*muTTayides*) will come to the house during that period and give her turmeric-vermillion and flowers, because she cannot use them after that. they also give her blouse pieces, betel-areca, money, anything except "scent." When the mourning period is over, she will neither give to nor take these things from *muTTayides*.

The visits can be at any time of the day. Visitors come on the fifth, seventh, and ninth days to give these things to her. (Or she may go out to visit others, or to her natal place, to receive these gifts.) She gives them the same things that they give her. When the women return to their homes, they take a bath, to remove the *mailige* that goes with the bereaved family's ritually polluted state (*sutaka*). *Mailige* can be washed off. *Sutaka* only goes with time.

The gifts from *muTTayides* are given on a plate, not a *moRa*. (We only use the winnowing fan to give things to Maramma beggars who come into our neighborhood.)

On the tenth day her mother's house gives her a sari. Formerly it was a red color sari, but now it can be any color. On this day the daughters of the house – only married daughters – should prepare

189

(y)eriappa, a collection of fried snacks, and *avalakki* for *puri-vunde*. Only married daughters can do this cooking. If there are no married daughters, it just is not done.

> Recipe: *avalakki*. Paddy is boiled for a while, and then soaked in the boiled water overnight. Strain off the water the next day. While the soaked paddy is still wet, fry it in a mud cooking pot (*bandle*) a little at a time. Then put it into a *varalu* and pound it with two pounding pestles (*haares*), to remove the husks. Two people must pound. Then separate out (*keerodu* 'separate') the husk (*hoTTu*) from the flattened rice, which is called *avalakki*.

> Recipe: *puri vunde*. Put sand into an iron cooking pan (*bandle*), and fry the *avalakki* in it. The sand should be very hot, the fire continuously burning. Firewood is best for this purpose, as it produces better heat than charcoal. Separate the rice *puri* from the sand in an *akki vandri*. Then make a thick syrup from jaggery (*bella*): it should be of a consistency, that a small drop sinks to the bottom.. Mix together roasted peanuts, dry coconut cut up in small pieces, roasted Bengal gram (*hurigaDle*). Mix these with the *puri* a little at a time, add syrup, and make balls. Roll with your hands, using some rice flour on your hands.

On the tenth day, relatives bring snacks (*tiNDi*) to the widow's house, for distribution on the 11th day. On the tenth day men will do a shaastra near the river, but women do not go outside at all. The widow's ceremony must be done in the morning, before 10a.m., when the men come back from the river. On this day, the woman, accompanied by another widow, takes off her *maagalya* (*taaLi*) herself, as she sits on the floor or a cot (*chapey*)[107], surrounded by all the plates of turmeric- vermillion, betel-areca, and so on, that she has received – there could be as many as 30 plates there. The other widow can sit anywhere in the room, next to her, in front of her, wherever. Her glass bangles also are removed, not broken. (In other castes the bangles are broken near the river by another woman.) No one else will be with them. The new sari that was presented to her will have been washed, and she puts it on.

Some change is occurring. If a woman is young when her husband dies, she prefers not to put on the new (washed) sari, but older women do put it on. The sari is washed because "Widows cannot wear new clothes." For this reason, a widowed mother will have her daughter wear a new sari before she puts it on.

Widows are invited on auspicious occasions, but just to watch, not to perform rituals. Even in olden times they were invited to see a God, take *mangalaarati*, and so on. They are called to bless a new couple and will be given betel-areca sets, but not turmeric and vermillion. (They actually do not chew the betel-areca.) The only ritual occasion requiring the help of a widow is this 10th day ceremony for another widow.

---

[107] She does not sit on a *hase maNe*. This is only for auspicious occasions.

Figure 59. An Elderly Widow Drying Her Red Sari Near the River, Bandipur 1966

Q: I have heard that widows should be careful to protect their purity (*maDi*), in order to protect their husbands' souls. Is that true here?

A: For us, we have no such belief. Whatever we do affects our own karma, not that of anyone else.

The only real change in widowhood from earlier times is that the woman's head is no longer shaved. And a widow is not required to wear a red sari.

ANNEX-4

FOLK TAXONOMY: PLANT CATEGORIES AND PLANT PARTS

In order to better understand how and why specific plant materials were required in these and other folk rituals, I set out to learn more about what the plants actually were, and how people thought about plants in general. Almost ten years after we completed our initial ethnographic study in Bandipur and Chinnapura, I made two two-month trips to Karnataka in 1976 and 1977 pursuing these questions. A Bangalore botanist, Father Cecil J. Saldanha, kindly helped with botanical identifications of plants of interest[108].

Several people told me about their botanical terms and categories. Detailed information on local plant knowledge and ideas came mostly from 18 Kannada-speaking individuals in 1976 and 1977. Fifteen of them were residents of the two Hassan District villages in which most of our field research was conducted, or of their hamlets. One was a resident of a nearby town; and two were from Mysore City. Thirteen were non-Brahmans, Scheduled Caste (A.K.), or Christian (one); and five were Brahmans. Eleven maintained farms, though only six of these were members of the Farmer (Okkaliga) caste. Seven supported

---

[108] In the summers of 1976 and 1977 I was able to do this ethnobotany study with support from the American Institute of Indian Studies and a Fulbright Faculty Research Abroad. Much of the initial data analysis was done in 1975 with a fellowship from the American Council of Learned Societies. This research was greatly helped by Ms. H. Malathi (later employed at the Central Food Technological Research Institute), who accompanied me as an interpreter and assistant. Mr. Malla Setty in 2022 provided me with some supplementary information.

themselves (or were in families supported) by other means, such as teaching, clerical work, retail business, or sooth-saying (one man). Some with their own farms also had businesses or salaried jobs. One young man, Mr. Malla Setty -- a former research assistant from our 1960s work -- had a bank job in the region and also managed a farm in his natal village. Another family had land and a tailoring business. They were also of the same Weaver caste background as Mr. Malla Setty. One young woman was a professional flower-seller whose parents earned their living as menial laborers.

These people contributed in different ways. The young flower-seller took me around village gardens as she eagerly told me about flowers and their qualities. Some others took me to their own backyards to show me plants. Two men brought me samples of nearly all the plants I was trying to identify, and one man escorted me around the village fields and discussed the names and features of plants we saw. Of these various methods, the walks proved the most informative and produced the most new information. Even in the months of July and August, when most plants are only beginning to sprout, I was able to learn much about folk botany when out with the plants themselves.

Categories of Plants

Beginning with the question, 'What are the types of plants?', I was told of nine or ten types. Five of these came readily when an individual heard the question; three more emerged when walking through village lands. The most commonly used expression for 'plants' in general is a two-word phrase *mara-giDagaLu*, which means literally 'trees-(and)-miscellaneous other plants'. The first six types of plants, mentioned in sit-down interviews, are as follow:

194

- *giDa* 'shrub'/'herbaceous plant'/'branch or twig'/'plant'

- *mara* 'tree'

- *podaru* 'shrub', an infrequently used term

- *baLLi* 'vine'/'creeper'

- *hullu* 'grass

Three additional categories were mentioned as we were in the presence of actual plants. These terms tend to be used as affixes to other words. That is, they refer to parts of plants that define the category. The three are

- *muLLu* 'thorny plant'

- *kaDDi* 'small woody plant'

- *kaLLi* (or *-gaLLi*) 'plant with milky sap'

The two last categories are not mutually exclusive. One small, woody plant with milky sap, for example, is called *kaDDi-kaLLi*.

A possible tenth category, labelled by an affix, is *hambu. Hambu* is a woody stem larger than *kaDDi* but much smaller than a tree. The Kannada name of one plant (*Sarcostemma brevistoma*) used to decorate village cattle during the Festival of Lights, includes this term: *moTuli hambu.*

195

Named Plant Parts

The Kannada way of describing plant structure reflects traditional understandings of growth and natural order. Its emphases are dynamic and growth-oriented. It directs one's attention to the activity and development of plants, rather than to their immobile nature. Shoots, leaves, and fruits have infancy, youth, maturity and old age clearly distinguished. This aspect of folk terminology presents a clear view of plants that is analogous to the cultural view of people's development, degeneration, and renewal; and it is clearly one key to the metaphorical uses of plants in folklore.

This point was made clear to me in 1966, when I made my first visit to the village fields of Bandipur to have a look at the most important food crops. My companion, P. Jayamma, an eighteen-year-old Farmer caste woman working as my assistant, asked me as we approached her farm, 'You know about *biija, moggu, huuvu, kaayi*, and *haNNu*, don't you?' I replied that I did not. She gave me a quick lesson in the stages of development of a plant, explaining that the 'seed' (*biija*) comes before the 'flower bud' (*moggu*), which in turn must precede the 'flower' (*huuvu*), 'green fruit' (*kaayi*), and 'ripe fruit' (*haNNu*) stages, after which the plant withers and produces more 'seeds'. Direct and simple as this was, it showed me once and for all how important growth is in the common Kannada understanding of the plant kingdom.

A plant is divided into named sections that are either below ground or above ground. (Figure 60) The portions below the ground are called *beeru* 'root' or *gaDDE* 'rhizome/bulb/corm'. (It is possible that a rhizome may sometimes be called 'root', but the distinction is usually maintained.) Thus, a potato, called *geDDE* (full name *aaLugeDDe*), is 'rhizome', while the root of a tree is *beeru* 'root'. Plants with rhizomes also have roots, and these are labelled as such. Turmeric, a plant whose rhizome is of universal ritual, medical, and culinary value, is generally called by its name (*arashiNa*) alone.

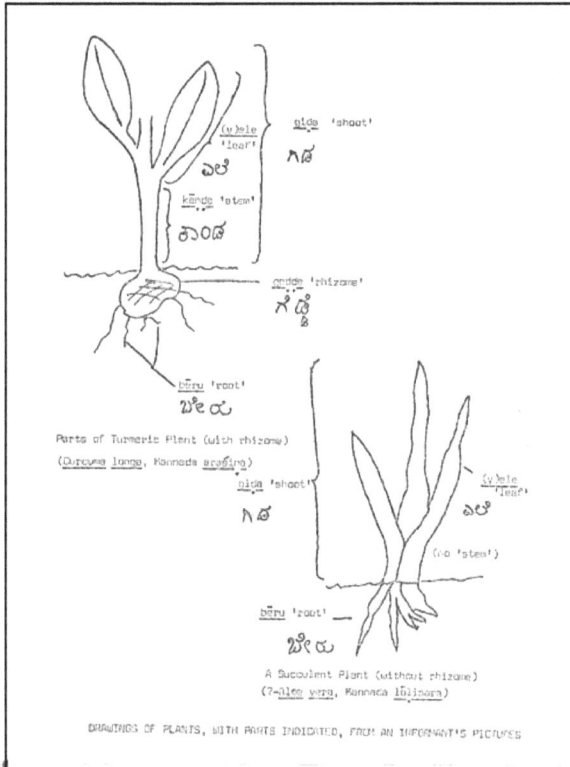

Figure 60. Named Parts of a Plant

In shrubs and herbaceous plants the portion above the ground is called *giDa*. Though divided terminologically into several parts (stem, branch, leaf, etc.), the visible portion of the plant as a whole is *giDa*. This word is the most flexibly used of all local plant terms. It can mean small 'shoot'; but it also can refer to a 'branch' or other another portion of a plant. If one picks off a branch of a fruiting or flowering bush, for example, one usually has hold of a *giDa*.

In trees there is a special term for the base of the trunk. It is *badde*. The term for the remainder of the trunk is the same as for the stem of a shrub or herbaceous plant: *kaaNDa* 'stem/trunk'. A synonym for 'stem' is *danTTu*. In lighter plants, the stem is covered with *sippe* 'skin'; and in most trees, with *togaTe* 'bark'. Inside the trunk of a tree is *mara* 'wood'. The term *mara* also refers to the entire tree.

Branches, large or small, are called *kombe/kombu* 'branch'.

Once having been removed from the tree (or fallen off), a branch becomes *koolu* 'stick', especially if leafless. A whole banana plant, cut off at its base to make an appearance at a village ritual is called *baaLe kamba*. *Kamba* also means 'post', as in a wooden house post.

A small, woody twig, fallen from a tree, is *kaDDi* 'twig'. A newly growing shoot which does not yet have leaves is called *tudi* 'tip'. Once it begins to sprout leaves, it is called *cigaru* 'new leaf shoot'

The term *(y)ele* 'leaf' refers to both petiole and leaf blade.

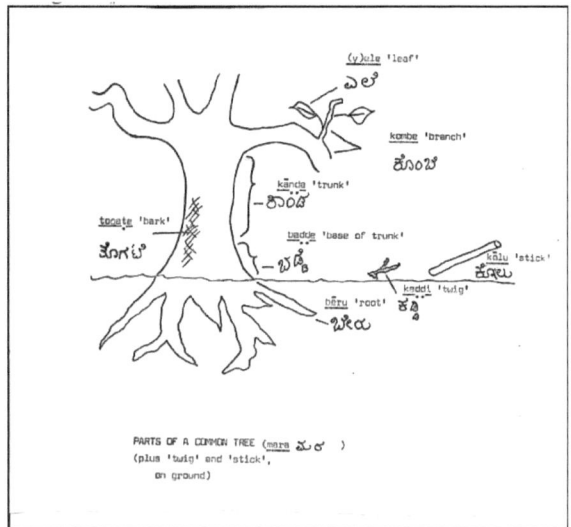

Figure 61. Named Parts of a Tree

There is no special word for the small stem supporting a leaf, that is, although there is a special word for the small stem supporting a flower (see below). The term *(y)ele* (unlike *soppu*) is reserved for the more sturdy types of leaves. A tripartite compound leaf is called *patre*. The fronds of a palm tree or a *Pandanus*, both monocotyledons, are not called 'leaves'. They are called *gari*. They are said to be composed of two parts, *diNDu* 'leaf stem' and *gari* 'leaflet'. Tree bark is referred to as *togaTe* if it is thick and hard, or as *sippe* if it is thin or soft.

A light, delicate leaf is a *soppu*, even when it is on a tree, such as the soap-nut (*siigemara*, actually a climbing prickly shrub, soapnut). All members of the *soppu* life form class have such leaves. The same term, *soppu*, can refer to a bunch of leaves.[109]

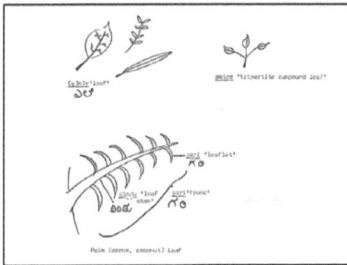

Figure 62. Types of Leaves

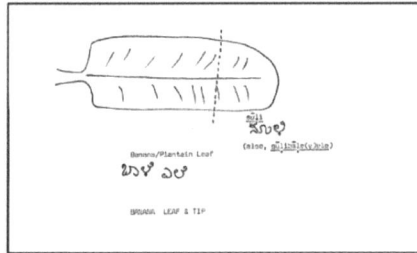

Figure 63. Plantain Leaf Parts

In the interviews conducted, I was unable to elicit a general term for tree 'sap', although there are a couple of terms for specific types of sap. This was a disappointment, in view of the importance of sap in literary allusions to plants in Indian mythology. There clearly is more to the subject than I have been able to discover. I was told of one Kannada term for 'milky sap': *sone*.

Plants that have this in them are sometimes found in village rituals. Dr. Regelson's field notes refer to a distinction between "white" and "black" sap, the latter being called *kaaLa haalu* 'black milk'. This distinction may be a matter of esoteric knowledge, and I

---

[109] Helen Ullrich, personal communication.

have no further information on it. (In common Tamil, the word for milky sap is *paal* 'milk'.)[110]

The second type of sap that is named is the sap of the toddy and coconut palms. Both of these are used to make liquor; and both have one name when fresh (*niira*) and another when fermented (*heNDa*). The fermentation process is said to be completed by noon, the fresh sap having been drained from the tree early in the morning.

The careful attention to different parts of a tree's trunk and to the branching process may reflect a metaphorical association between trees and human families. The same man who told me about the term for 'base of (a tree) trunk' in 1976 had told me ten years earlier that a group of agnatic relatives who are distantly related to each other share a common *badde* group. They are relatives, he had explained, but they no longer know exactly how they are related.

The Kannada terminology itself focuses on the budding and branching process in the terms for 'tip' or 'new shoot', both giving rise to 'branch'. In general there are ways for Kannada speakers to emphasize the forward ends of both branch and leaf. The word most commonly used for the 'forward end' is *kone*, literally 'an extremity'.

This term is applied to branches when requiring the end of a branch for a ritual; and it is also applied to the turmeric rhizome, which is used whole for some rituals: *arasiNa kone*. One informant insists that one can only use this term for turmeric in its whole, natural, uncut form. In one Brahman ritual, in which a turmeric rhizome is used to inscribe a new baby's name in a dish of raw rice, it is called *arasiNada kombu*, a phrase that uses one of the words for 'branch'.

---

[110] Margaret Trawick Egnor, personal communication

The forward tip of the banana leaf has a special name. It is called *suuLi*. This is a necessary element of ritual meals, such as those served to ancestors. Considered the best part, it is the only suitable plate for such meals; though the rest of the leaf will do at most other times. In the wider context of this folk botany, these specially named forward ends, whether root, rhizome, leaf, or branch, acquire the connotations of both culmination and energetic growth, an "auspicious" state of being.

In a system where branching terminology is a detailed part of folk botany, it is interesting that palms, which tend not to branch, are a separate category. The leaves and flowers of palm trees are called by different names than the leaves and flowers of other plants. (*Pandanus*, also a monocotyledon, has the same leaf name as palms but the same word for 'flower' as other plants.) Coconut or areca leaves are called *gari* 'frond'; and their flowers are called *hombaaLe*[111]. These flowers resemble each other. They are inflorescences consisting of thirty or forty branches that can be up to 18 inches in length, each covered with 200-300 little flowers and nubby baby fruits. The inflorescences are borne in leaf axils of plants that are at least five years old.

A palm frond grows out of a sheath, actually a large, tough spathe. This also has a special name: *paTTe* 'spathe'. One person I interviewed drew a picture of it for me (See Figure 64).

---

[111] I also have heard the areca flower referred to simply as 'areca flower' – *aDike huuvu*. But *hombaaLe* was more often used.

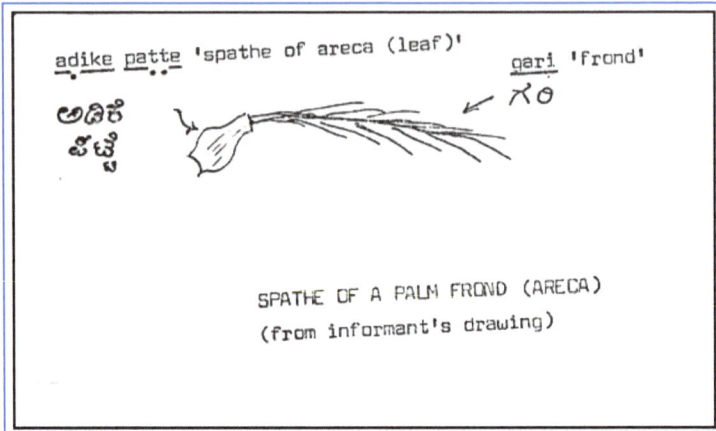

Figure 64. Spathe of a Palm Frond

The term for 'flower or leaf bud' is *moggu*. We also heard the term *moLake* used to refer to a newly 'sprouted' leaf. Flowers are all called *huuvu*, except for coconut and areca flowers, which are referred to by different terms.[112] A 'flower' includes the corolla or petals – called *huuvin(y)eslu*, *(y)esalu*, or *reke* – and a central portion, called *kusumi* or *kusuma*, 'carpels and stamens'.[113] This central portion is the place where seeds develop 'after the flower gets old and useless' (*haaLehoogaavaga*). The calyx (sepals), part of the supporting structure, is called *toTTu* or *kaDDi* 'flower petiole'.

During interviews in which people explained these matters to me, they often used specific plants and flowers to demonstrate points of flower anatomy. These illustrations sometimes produced further information. A detail of flower structure that was often used to distinguish types was whether petals were arranged in a single or a multiple 'round'. The hibiscus flower (*H. rosa-sinensis*), for example, is

---

[112] According to Bhat (1968-70), *kusuma* is another Kannada term for 'flower'. But this term was not used in our study area.

[113] According to Helen Ullrich (personal communication), *kusuma* also may refer to an entire flower.

a flower that has only a 'single round' (*(v)ondsuTTindu*). The popular *sugandharaaja*, called "tube rose" in English, was used as an example of a flower that has no supporting petiole (*toTTu*). This same plant was used to demonstrate that some flowers grow in clusters (*gonchilu* 'cluster') rather than singly.

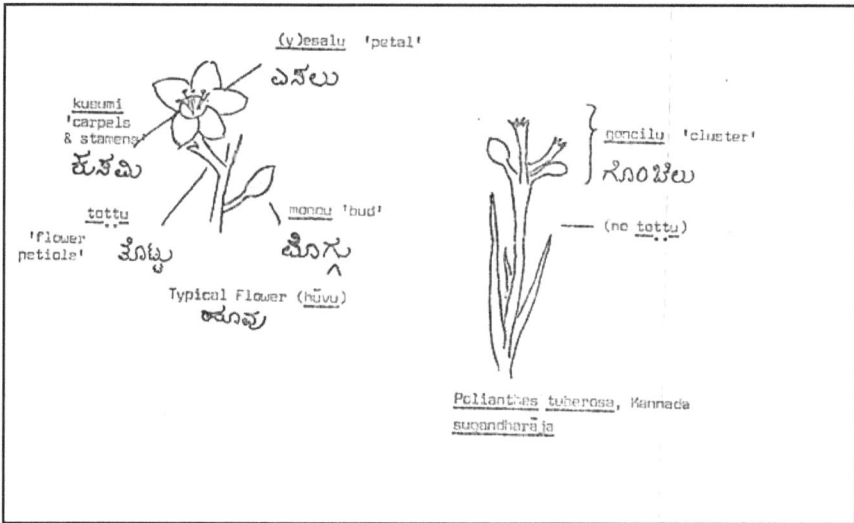

Figure 65. Named Parts of a Flower

Distinguishing a single flower from a 'cluster' or a single round of petals from a multiple round, and perhaps also a single leaf from a (tripartite) compound leaf, these aspects of Kannada ethnobotany are consonant with the larger cultural framework, which carefully distinguishes auspicious occasions/items/images from inauspicious ones. Life and energetic (Kannada *šubhakara*) activity are 'auspicious'. Death and funerary rituals are 'inauspicious' (Kannada *ašubha*). This central concept has a numerical side to it. Singularity is often considered 'inauspicious' while multiplicity is seen as 'auspicious'. This distinction applies in rituals; and it influences decorative art, which typically uses multiple colors and busy designs throughout South Asia.

The fact that singularity distinguished from multiplicity therefore makes a certain kind of sense in South Asian folk science that it might not in some other world regions. (Hanchett 2023; Carman and Marglin 1985)

As I mentioned earlier, the process of fruit maturation is divided into stages, of which the flower is one. When a fruit is very small and young, it is called *hiichu* or *ichchu* 'baby fruit'. While green and developing, it is called *kaayi* 'green fruit/vegetable'. Many food crops are eaten while in this phase of development. As fruits ripen, they are called *haNNu* 'fruit'. For example, the plaintain or banana in its green phase is called *baaLekaayi*; and in its ripe, sweet phase, *baaLehaNNu*.

Over-ripe fruit is *haaL-* 'old/spoiled/useless': this is the phase of seed production. The local term for 'seed' is *biija* (borrowed from Sanskrit); and the cycle continues, as seeds give rise to new plants with 'buds', 'flowers', and their 'baby fruits'.

The parts of an edible fruit in Kannada folk taxonomy are simple to describe. A fruit consists of a *sippe*, 'skin' on the outside; *haNNu*, 'fruit' on the inside; and *biijagaLu,* 'seeds'.

Repeating the theme of multiplicity, there is a special term for the sections of a fruit, such as jackfruit, which has more than one section inside. It is *tooLe* 'fruit section'. The jackfruit whole is called *haNNu*; but this term is not used to refer to the sections, which are the parts eaten.

ANNEX-5

TRANSCRIPTION OF KANNADA
WORDS

Short vowels are transcribed with single letters: *a, i, e, o, u*

Long vowels are transcribed with double letters: *aa, ii, ee, oo, uu*

Retroflex consonants are transcribed with capital letters: *D, N, T, L*

Short/Long VOWELS	
Kannada	Transcription
ಅ	a
ಆ	aa
ಇ	i
ಈ	ii
ಒ	o
ಓ	oo
ಎ	e
ಏ	ee
ಉ	u
ಊ	uu

Retroflex Consonants: N,D,T,L	
Kannada	Transcription
ಣ	Na
ಡ	Da
ಟ್	T
ಳ	La

ANNEX-6

GLOSSARY OF BOTANICAL AND KANNADA PLANT NAMES

Glossary of Botanical and Kannada Plant Names

Botanical Name	Botanical Family	Kannada Name (transcribed)	Kannada Script	English Name	Used in Family Rituals or Tabooed (*) [1]
Abelmoschus esculentis	Malvaceae	beNDekaayi	ಬೆಂಡೆಕಾಯಿ	Okra/Lady's finger	7(*)
Achyranthes aspera L.	Amaranthaceae	uttaraNi	ಉತ್ತರಣಿ		3
Acorus calamus	Acoraceae	bhaje	ಭಜೆ	Sweet flag	1
Areca catechu Linn.	Palmae	aDike	ಅಡಿಕೆ	Areca	1,3,4,4
Artocarpus heterophyllus Lam.	Moraceae/Arto-carpaceae	halasina haNNu, -mara, -giDa	ಹಲಸಿನ ಹಣ್ಣು, -ಮರ, -ಗಿಡ	Jackfruit	2,3
Acadirachta indica A. Juss.	Meliaceae	beevu, beevin-soppu, beevinamara	ಬೇವು, ಬೇವಿನಸೊಪ್ಪು, ಬೇವಿನ ಮರ	Neem	3,8
Bambusa arundinaceae (Retz.) Roxburgh	Gramineae/Bambu-saceae/Poaceae	bidiru, bambu	ಬಿದಿರು, ಬಂಬು	Bamboo	3

[1] 1-Birth/naming, 2-Girl's Maturation, 3-Boys Initiation, 4-Marriage, 5-Pregnancy, 6-Death, 7-Ancestor Propitiation, 8-Pujas for fierce goddesses

Glossary of Botanical and Kannada Plant Names (2)

Botanical Name	Botanical Family	Kannada Name (transcribed)	Kannada Script	English Name	Used in Family Rituals or Tabooed (*)
Butea monosperma (Lam.) Kuntze	Fabaceae	muttugada mara muttugada kone	ಮುತ್ತುಗದ ಮರ ಮುತ್ತುಗದಕೊನೆ	Bastard teak tree -branch tip	3
Cajanus cajan (L.) Millspaugh	Leguminosae /Fabaceae	togari – kaayi togari - beeLe togari - kaaLu	ತೊಗರಿಕಾಯಿ ತೊಗರಿಬೇಳೆ ತೊಗರಿಕಾಳು	Tur Daal Split bean Whole bean	4
Calotropis gigantea (L.) R.Br.	Apocynaceae	(y)ekkada-huuvu (y)ekkada-giDa	ಎಕ್ಕದಕುವ್ವ ಎಕ್ಕದಗಿಡ	Crown flower Milkweed	1,3,8
Cassia fistula L.	Leguminosae /Fabaceae	kakke giDa (plant) kakke huuvu (flower)	ಕಕ್ಕೆ ಗಿಡ ಕಕ್ಕೆ ಕುವ್ವ	Golden shower tree	1,3,6
Chrysanthemum indicum	Compositae	saavantige huuvu	ಸಾವಂತಿಗೆಕುವ್ವ	Chrysanthemum flower	6,7
Butea monosperma (Lam.) Kuntze	Fabaceae	muttugada mara muttugada kone	ಮುತ್ತುಗದ ಮರ ಮುತ್ತುಗದಕೊನೆ	Bastard teak tree -branch tip	3
Cajanus cajan (L.) Millspaugh	Leguminosae /Fabaceae	togari – kaayi togari - beeLe togari - kaaLu	ತೊಗರಿಕಾಯಿ ತೊಗರಿಬೇಳೆ ತೊಗರಿಕಾಳು	Tur Daal Split bean Whole bean	4

Glossary of Botanical and Kannada Plant Names (4)

Botanical Name	Botanical Family	Kannada Name (transcribed)	Kannada Script	English Name	Used in Family Rituals or Tabooed (*)
Cucurbita spp.	Cucurbitaceae	kambalakaayi	ಕಂಬಳಕಾಯಿ	Pumpkin	7(*)
Cynodon dactylon Pers. Syn. Agrostis linearis Retz.	Gramineae	garika, garike	ಗರಿಕ ಗರಿಕೆ	Bermuda grass	3,4
Eleusine coracana	Poaceae	raagi	ರಾಗಿ	Finger millet	1,4
Ficus glomerata Roxb.	Moraceae	attimara	ಅತ್ತಿಮರ	Country fig tree	2,4,5
Ficus indica L.	Moraceae	aaladamara	ಆಲದಮರ	Banyan tree	3,5,6
Ficus religiosa L.	Moraceae	araLimara	ಅರಳಿಮರ	Sacred fig/pipal tree	3,4,5,6
Hibiscus rosa-sinensis Linn.	Malvaceae	daasavaLada-huuvu	ದಾಸವಾಳದಹೂವು		6
Jasminium spp.	Oleaceae	malligehuuvu kaakaDahuuvu	ಮಲ್ಲಿಗೆಹೂವು ಕಾಕಡ ಹೂವು	Jasmine	6
Lagenaria siseraria	Cucurbitaceae	sorekaayi	ಸೋರೆಕಾಯಿ	Bottle gourd	7(*)
Leucas indica R.Br. (Leucas aspera)	Lamiaceae /Labiatae	tumbehuuvu tumbegiDa kasitumbe	ತುಂಬೆಹೂವು ತುಂಬೆಗಿಡ ಕಾಸಿತುಂಬ	Common leucas -small size -bigger size	4,6

208

Glossary of Botanical and Kannada Plant Names (5)

Botanical Name	Botanical Family	Kannada Name (transcribed)	Kannada Script	English Name	Used in Family Rituals or Tabooed (*)
Luffa acutangula (L.) Roxb.	Cucurbitaceae	hiirekaayi	ಹೀರೆಕಾಯಿ	Ridge gourd	7(*)
Macronloma uniflorum Lam.	Fabaceae	huraLi kaaLu	ಹುರಳಿ ಕಾಳು	Horse gram	1,4
Mangifera indica L	Anacardiaceae	maavinamara maavinahaNNu maavintuyele	ಮಾವಿನಮರ ಮಾವಿನಹಣ್ಣು ಮಾವಿನೆಲೆ	Mango tree Mango fruit Mango leaf	1,2,6
Momordica charantia	Cucurbitaceae	haagalakaayi	ಹಾಗಲಕಾಯಿ	Bitter gourd	7
Musa sapientum L.	Musaceae	baaLe - -haNNu -kaayi -mara -giDa	ಬಾಳೆ ಬಾಳೆಹಣ್ಣು ಬಾಳೆಕಾಯಿ ಬಾಳೆಮರ ಬಾಳೆ ಗಿಡ	Plantain -ripe fruit -unripe -tree -plant	1,4,6,7
Myristica fragrans		jaayikaayi	ಜಾಯಿಕಾಯಿ	Nutmeg	1,2
Nerium indicum Miller	Apocynaceae	kaNigale huuvu	ಕಣಿಗಲೆ ಹೂವು	Oleander	6,8

209

Glossary of Botanical and Kannada Plant Names (6)

Botanical Name	Botanical Family	Kannada Name (transcribed)	Kannada Script	English Name	Used in Family Rituals or Tabooed (*)
Ocymum sanctum L.	Labiatae	tuLasi	ತುಳಸಿ	Sacred basil	6
Oryza sativa Linn.	Gramineae	bhatta akki anna akshate	ಭತ್ತ ಅಕ್ಕಿ ಅನ್ನ ಅಕ್ಷತೆ	Rice paddy Raw rice Cooked rice Raw rice mixed with turmeric	1,2,3,4,6,7
Phaseolus aureus Roxb.	Fabaceae/Legumi-nosae	hesaru beeLe	ಹೆಸರುಬೇಳೆ	Green gram (split)	4,6
Phaseolus mungo Linn.	Leguminosae/Fabaceae	uddu uddinabeeLe uddinakaaLu	ಉದ್ದು ಉದ್ದಿನಬೇಳೆ ಉದ್ದಿನಕಾಳು	Black gram Split pulse Whole bean	4
Piper betle		viLyadele	ವೀಳ್ಯದೆಲೆ	Betel leaf	1,2,4,6
Plumeria rubra L. forma acuminata (Ait.) Sant. & Irani ex Shah	Apocynaceae	deya-kaNigale huuvu[1]	ದೇಯ-ಕಣಿಗಲೆಹೂವು	Plumeria	8

1. Ramaswami & Razi, *Flora of Bangalore*, call this "*devagaNigLu.*"

Glossary of Botanical and Kannada Plant Names (7)

Botanical Name	Botanical Family	Kannada Name (transcribed)	Kannada Script	English Name	Used in Family Rituals or Tabooed (*)
Poa cynosuroides Retz. [Synonym: Erogrostis cynosuroides]	Graminaceae /Poaceae	darbhe (or) darbha	ದರ್ಭೆ ದರ್ಭ		3,6
Ricinus communis L.	Euphorbiaceae	haraLu (or) haLLu haraLeNNe	ಹರಳು ಹಳ್ಳು ಹರಳೆಣ್ಣೆ	Castor Castor oil	1
Saccharum arundinaceum Retz.	Gramineae	kabbu, sakare bella	ಕಬ್ಬು ಸಕರೆ ಬೆಲ್ಲ	Sugar cane Sugar Jaggery	1,2,3,4,6
Santalum album	Santalaceae	srigandha	ಶ್ರೀಗಂಧ	Sandalwood	6
Securinega leucopyrus (Willd.) Müll. Arg. [Synonym: Flueggea leuco-pyrus Willd.]	Phyllanthaceae	hulikaDDi (stick)	ಹುಲಿಕಡ್ಡಿ		6

211

Glossary of Botanical and Kannada Plant Names (8)

Botanical Name	Botanical Family	Kannada Name (transcribed)	Kannada Script	English Name	Used in Family Rituals or Tabooed (*)
Sesamum indicum Linn.	Pedaliaceae	(t)eLLu, kari(t)eLLu, puTTeLLu	ಎಳ್ಳು ಕರಿಎಳ್ಳು ಬಿಳಿಎಳ್ಳು	Sesame, Black sesame, Sesame	2,4,6
Solanum melongena	Solanaceae	badane, badanekaayi, badanegiDa	ಬದನೆ ಬದನೆಕಾಯಿ ಬದನೆಗಿಡ	Brinjal /Eggplant, -vegetable, -plant	7
Solanum nigrum	Solanaceae	gaaNike huuvu	ಗಾಣಿಕೆ ಹೂವು		6
Solanum tuberosum	Solanaceae	aalugeDDe	ಆಲುಗಡ್ಡೆ	Potato	7
Sorghum bicolor	Poaceae	jooLa (or) navaNe	ಜೋಳ ನವಣೆ	Sorghum	2
Togetes erecta	Compositae	chenDuuvu	ಚೆಂಡುಹೂವು	Marigold	6
Tamarindus indica L.	Caesalpiniaceae /Leguminosae	huNisemara, huNisekaayi, huNisehaNNu	ಹುಣಿಸೆಮರ ಹುಣಿಸೆಕಾಯಿ ಹುಣಿಸೆಹಣ್ಣು	Tamarind tree, - fruit (unripe), -fruit (ripe)	1,2,6

Glossary of Botanical and Kannada Plant Names (9)

Botanical Name	Botanical Family	Kannada Name (transcribed)	Kannada Script	English Name	Used in Family Rituals or Tabooed (*)
Thevetia peruviana (Pers.) K.Schum.	Apocynaceae	*baalasampige-huuvu*	ಬಾಲಸಂಪಿಗೆಹೂವು		8(*)
Triticum aestivum	Poaceae	*goodhi* *rave* *(or) suji*	ಗೂಧಿ ರವೆ ಸುಜಿ	Wheat Granulated wheat/Semolina	4
Vigna catjang Walp.	Fabaceae /Papilionaceae	*taDaguNikaavi* (fresh), *taDNikaaLu* (dried)	ತಡಗುನಿಕಾವಿ ತಡ್ನಿಕಾಳು	A type of bean	2
Vitex negundo L.	Verbenaceae	*lakke* *-giDa* *-soppu*	ಲಕ್ಕೆ -ಗಿಡ -ಸೊಪ್ಪು	Five-leaved chaste tree -Plant -Leaf	Subject of a Kannada proverb or saying
Unknown i.d.		*bommmara*	ಬಮ್ಮಮರ	(some kind of palm)	3

213

Author Biographies

Suzanne Hanchett is a social anthropologist with a Ph.D. from Columbia University. She taught for ten years at Queens College of the City University of New York, Bard College, and Barnard College. In 1979 she started working as an applied and practicing anthropologist in New York City. In 1991 she began working as an international development consultant. Her specialties as an applied anthropologist are reproductive health, women's rights in development, drinking water quality, and sanitation. She retired in 2016 and now serves as Co-Chair of the International Women's Anthropology Conference (IWAC), an NGO accredited at the United Nations.

Stanley Regelson (1934-2016) was an anthropological linguist with a Ph.D. from Columbia University. He taught anthropology at the State University of New York, Stony Brook, and at Lehman College of the City University of New York. He also had a long career in New York City government, retiring in 2014.

Stanley Regelson and Suzanne Hanchett in Karnataka, 1967

K. Gurulingaiah has a M.A. degree in Sociology from Mysore University, and Bachelors and Masters degrees in Library & Informational Science. He did many of the in-depth interviews used in this book. He is retired from a career in library science and now lives in Bengaluru.

K. Gurulingaiah, 1967

Index

amma deities, 143

Areca nut, 25, 48, 57, 88, 123

Auspicious or Inauspicious
occasions, 12, 24, 45, 60, 61,
62, 67, 70, 96, 99, 121, 122,
148, 150, 151, 152, 153, 154,
159, 161, 169, 191, 201, 203

Ayurveda, 8, 9, 94

Betel leaf, 31, 34, 36, 38, 57, 61,
67, 68, 73, 77, 91, 94, 149, 150

Betel-areca, 15, 109, 121, 123,
126, 150

Burial, 99, 100, 104, 106, 109,
110, 114, 116, 117, 121, 123,
124, 125, 126, 146, 148, 149,
150, 152, 154, 155, 158

Cassia fistula, 17, 25, 43, 52, 55,
106, 124, 156, 162

Castes

Barber, 14, 20, 40, 42, 44, 45,
46, 51, 52, 53, 54, 55, 60,
66, 68, 72, 73, 78, 82, 84,
85, 89, 90, 92, 100, 103,
124, 153, 156, 158, 160,
162, 163, 164, 187

Farmer, 14, 15, 17, 20, 21, 22,
27, 29, 30, 31, 32, 33, 36,
37, 38, 39, 40, 41, 42, 45,
54, 55, 58, 60, 61, 62, 64,
65, 66, 74, 75, 82, 86, 91,
93, 94, 95, 96, 97, 98, 100,
102, 120, 138, 139, 148,
152, 153, 156, 158, 160,
162, 163, 187, 193, 196

Fisherman, 14, 19, 21, 23, 25,
29, 30, 31, 39, 60, 72, 93,

95, 100, 105, 106, 110, 114,
120, 124, 125, 126, 127,
160, 187, 188

Iyengar Brahman, 4, 14, 16,
17, 23, 24, 25, 26, 27, 40,
41, 46, 47, 48, 50, 56, 57,
60, 61, 70, 71, 74, 75, 77,
78, 83, 85, 87, 88, 89, 92,
93, 94, 96, 98, 99, 100, 118,
119, 120, 124, 126, 146,
148, 149, 152, 160, 161,
163, 180, 187, 189

Oil Presser, 14, 100, 101, 104,
106, 109, 123, 124, 125,
126, 127, 141, 146, 155,
156, 158, 187

Scheduled Caste, 14, 15, 18,
19, 20, 23, 24, 28, 29, 30,
31, 33, 34, 35, 36, 37, 38,
39, 40, 41, 45, 58, 59, 60,
62, 82, 83, 93, 95, 99, 100,
102, 104, 106, 110, 112,
119, 125, 126, 129, 130,
132, 139, 146, 150, 153,
159, 161, 164, 166, 187, 193

Shepherd, 60, 62, 66, 68, 71,
74, 84, 90, 91, 149, 157, 187

Smartha Brahman, 14, 16, 26,
29, 34, 40, 41, 46, 58, 60,
61, 70, 71, 79, 89, 93, 94,
96, 97, 100, 103, 105, 111,
118, 120, 124, 125, 126,
127, 146, 154, 160, 163, 187

Smith, 14, 22, 23, 24, 29, 30,
32, 40, 41, 46, 50, 52, 54,
55, 56, 57, 60, 61, 71, 84,

88, 93, 97, 99, 100, 117,
125, 126, 149, 152, 156,
160, 163, 166, 187
Washerman, 14, 21, 40, 42, 43,
54, 55, 60, 100, 103, 120,
156, 162, 187
Weaver, 14, 60, 78, 130, 142,
187, 194
Cicer arietinum, 26, 37, 56, 89,
97, 124, 152, 160, 170
Coconut
tender, 89, 124
Coconuts, 7, 32, 57, 82, 89, 97,
124, 134, 146, 151, 183, 201
Cynodon dactylon, 48, 56, 60,
90, 161
Daas sect, 14, 22, 24, 40, 41, 45,
54, 55, 60, 100, 112, 120, 145,
149, 151, 152, 153, 156, 162,
163, 166, 171, 187
Flower
Coconut, 146
Flowers
areca or coconut, 16, 26, 42,
54, 67, 70, 86, 88, 111, 121,
124, 151, 201
Calotropis gigantea, 17, 25,
51, 55, 141, 143, 156, 157
coconut, 146
deyya kaNigal (Plumeria), 143,
156, 157
kaNigal (see also *Nerium
indicum*), 126, 141, 143,
156
Ghosts, 99, 100, 105, 111, 118,
122, 123, 158, 170
Grains (see also
Seeds), 88, 92, 159
Jackfruit, 168
Jaggery, 27, 57, 123
Lagenaria siseraria, 134, 135,

158
Lap-filling ritual, 33
Leaves, 25, 27, 55, 125, 126
Leucas indica, 4, 66, 83, 84, 86,
91, 105, 106, 109, 121, 123,
125, 126, 156, 157, 158, 164,
170
Luffa acutangular, 131, 135, 158
Mango leaf strand over front
entrance for auspicious
occasions, 154
Mango leaves, 57, 87, 154
Marital pendant
taaLi, 5, 45, 46, 70, 77, 79, 81,
83, 89, 116, 120, 129, 164,
191
Medical uses of plants (see also
Ayurveda), 9, 170, 175, 180,
181, 182, 183, 185
Momordica charantia, 130, 134
Mull sect, 17, 22, 60, 62, 68, 73,
74, 75, 84, 86, 88, 91, 100,
102, 106, 112, 120, 123, 127,
156, 160, 164, 187
Nerium indicum, 115, 126, 141,
143, 156, 157
Nutmeg, 36
Outdoor shrine or canopy
pandal, 46, 71
Parijata, 3
Plantains, 7, 57, 98, 135, 148
Pounding grains or paddy, 66,
86, 91, 160
Pulses, 21, 46, 47, 51, 84, 85, 88
Bengal gram, 16, 17, 24, 25,
26, 31, 32, 35, 36, 37, 39,
47, 48, 52, 56, 61, 62, 68,
77, 79, 84, 85, 87, 88, 89,
92, 94, 95, 97, 104, 105,
112, 114, 121, 124, 130,
134, 145, 148, 152, 158,

160, 170, 190
Phaseolus aureus, 88, 92, 126
Purification, 176
Rice, 7, 10, 32, 98, 100, 126,
129, 131, 133, 135, 137, 152,
153, 154, 169, 179, 190
Ritual specialists
aynoru, 20
daasayya, 21, 43, 44, 45, 56,
117
priests, 12, 22, 53, 58, 115
Sacred basil plant, 12, 22, 101,
109, 124, 126, 155, 158
Seeds
scsamc, 39, 98, 123, 160
Seeds (see also
Grains), 92
Solanum nigrum, 101, 125, 127,
155
Sugar, 15, 16, 23, 27, 32, 50, 92
Trees
banyan, 7, 98
country fig, 98

jackfruit, 168
mango, 7, 57, 87, 154
neem, 143
sacred fig, 3, 6, 7, 51, 90, 98,
125, 160, 163, 182
Turmeric, 7, 32, 56, 77, 91, 97,
148, 197
Water, 21, 76, 90, 109, 180
river, 192
Water - pots of, to witness a
marriage, 62, 64, 84, 86, 88,
90, 91, 149, 153, 157, 160
Women
married, 110, 129
widows, 159, 191, 192
Wood
branches sticks and twigs, 55,
109, 121, 125, 127, 158,
161, 195, 198
bamboo, 7
Butea monosperma, 7, 55,
162, 164, 167

www.ingramcontent.com/pod-product-compliance
Lightning Source LLC
Chambersburg PA
CBHW040935030426
42335CB00001B/1